Be Happy.
Be Calm.
Be YOU.

A MINDFULNESS JOURNAL
for TEENS

Sara Katherine

ADAMS MEDIA
New York London Toronto Sydney New Delhi

Aadamsmedia

Adams Media
An Imprint of Simon & Schuster, Inc.
100 Technology Center Drive
Stoughton, MA 02072

First Adams Media trade paperback edition January 2021

ADAMS MEDIA and colophon are trademarks of Simon & Schuster.

For information about special discounts for bulk purchases, please contact Simon & Schuster Special Sales at 1-866-506-1949 or business@simonandschuster.com.

The Simon & Schuster Speakers Bureau can bring authors to your live event. For more information or to book an event contact the Simon & Schuster Speakers Bureau at 1-866-248-3049 or visit our website at www.simonspeakers.com.

Interior design, illustrations, and hand lettering by Priscilla Yuen

Manufactured in the United States of America

2 2022

Library of Congress Cataloging-in-Publication Data has been applied for.

ISBN 978-1-5072-1553-1

Contains material adapted from the following title published by Adams Media, an Imprint of Simon & Schuster, Inc.: *Stop. Breathe. Chill.* by Beth Stebner, copyright © 2016, ISBN 978-1-4405-9439-7.

CONTENTS

 introduction 8

CHAPTER 1 10

BE PRESENT WHILE YOU HANG:
Friendships and Relationships

CHAPTER 2 56

BRING MINDFULNESS HOME:
Family and Spaces

CHAPTER 3 88

KEEP CALM AND STUDY ON:
School

CHAPTER 4 130

STAY CENTERED AND HAPPY:
Self-Esteem and Self-Care

CHAPTER 5 180

WELCOME WHAT'S AHEAD:
Your Bright Future

INTRODUCTION

Being a teenager is stressful.

Whether you're dealing with pressure from your teachers and parents, balancing your crazy schedule with homework, cramming for exams, trying to excel at sports, managing friend drama, or filling out college applications...stress is everywhere.

So, how do *you* handle all this stress?

Do you procrastinate and scroll through TikTok when you're supposed to be studying? If you get in a fight with your friend, do you give her the silent treatment and hope it'll work itself out on its own? Are you constantly arguing with your parents about their rules and questions about your personal life?

If any of these sound like you, or if you're struggling to handle everything life is throwing your way, there's good news: This book will teach you productive ways to deal with stress *and* help your mind, body, and heart. (If you're coping with stress with candy, coffee drinks, and mental thunderstorms, you've only been making your physical and mental situation worse.) You'll practice self-care—you'll stop freaking out for a minute, ask yourself how you feel by checking in with your body and emotions, and then listen to your body so you can give it what it needs.

Another key concept you'll learn in *Be Happy. Be Calm. Be YOU.* is how to practice mindfulness, which simply means having a conscious awareness of the present moment. Instead of replaying an old fight in your head or worrying about next Friday's test, you'll just focus on today, on right now. Throughout this book, you'll find ideas on how to implement mindfulness in all aspects of your life. Each of the more than one hundred entries outlines a common stress-inducing topic, gives you suggestions on how to address it mindfully, then offers an affirmation you can recite to embrace a positive mindset. (Affirmations are powerful sentences that help you concentrate on positive thoughts and actions.) You can skip around the book to find help on the issues you're dealing with right now, or you can read through the whole book to get a wide range of ideas. And the activities and journal prompts are easy to fit in once a day, at any time that works for you.

Self-care and mindfulness won't cure all your stress over-night, of course—but like anything else, the more you practice, the more natural it will feel and the quicker you'll be able to recenter yourself. These practices also can't promise that you'll never encounter stress again—after all, our world is constantly changing, and with those changes will come different chal-lenges that may bring new types of stress into your life—but having solid self-care and mindfulness routines will help you understand how to tackle these new challenges and come out even stronger and happier than before.

The more you practice self-care and mindfulness, the less stressed you'll feel, and the happier, calmer, and more YOU you'll feel!

Let's get started! ⟳→

CHAPTER 1

BE PRESENT WHILE YOU HANG:
Friendships and Relationships

*Anything is possible when you have the
right people there to support you.*

—Misty Copeland, ballet dancer

Your friends are the most important people in your life. It makes
sense! You spend most of your weekdays together—sitting in class,
sharing lunches, participating in study sessions—plus you see each
other even more often if you do the same activities or sports or
hang out on weekends. And when you're not together? You're probably checking in, texting, FaceTiming, or Snapchatting constantly.

Through all this time and connection, you start to form deep emotional bonds with your friends, so of course these relationships become important to you. You likely even confide in your friends some thoughts and emotions you'd never share with your family. But making memories comes with both the fun times and inside jokes *and* some stressful times too. One habit you can build to help navigate all these ups and downs? Mindfulness.

Practicing mindfulness within your friendships and relationships will have a massive positive impact when it comes to taking care of your mental health, building stronger relationships with others (both as friends and romantically), and working on your relationship with yourself. In this chapter, you'll work through prompts and activities to help you through situations such as:

- Trying to become a better friend
- Arguments with your friends
- Dating someone you really like
- Moments when you're feeling lonely
- Experiencing heartache from a breakup or losing a friend
- And more

If you're ready to improve your friendships, develop romantic relationships, and learn to love yourself the way you truly deserve, you're in the right place! After completing this chapter, you'll be well on your way to inviting mindfulness into these special areas of your life. Applying these tools will empower you to live your life to the fullest!

Be the Kind of Friend You Want to Have

Friends make bad days better, give you someone to talk to or text with after class, and help you make hilarious memories that will last a lifetime. Plus, they can tell you if you've been walking around with toilet paper stuck to your shoe or broccoli wedged in your teeth because, hey, we've all been there. But maintaining a friendship takes time and effort, and to have friends, you first have to be the kind of person who will attract them. How do you do that? Think of the traits and qualities you want in a friend—maybe someone who's fiercely loyal or a good listener—and try practicing those traits in all your relationships.

YOUR TURN

What types of qualities are you looking for in a friend? Are you looking for someone who's honest, funny, loyal, or kind? Think about how you want to feel when you're hanging out and talking to each other for hours on end and build traits off of those feelings.

Take a moment to think about those qualities, then answer the following questions:

- Do you have any of these qualities now? Circle or add stars in the list you created next to the qualities you have yourself.
- Are there any qualities you want to have in the future? If yes, write about how you'd feel if you were to become a friend with your desired traits. How would you act? How would it improve your life? You can use the template provided on the next page.

QUALITIES I'M LOOKING FOR IN A FRIEND

 I would like to work on becoming more _____

_____ (QUALITY YOU WANT),

and I would feel _____

_____ (EMOTION).

I will start by _____

_____ (ACTION STEP).

◆◆◆ AFFIRMATION ◆◆◆

*Friendship is a reflection of who I am, so to have friends,
I first need to be a friend.*

Listen Carefully

On your mission to become a better friend, it's important to remember that everyone is dealing with something, whether you know about it or not. Maybe it's a bad grade in biology, or maybe life at home is stressful. If one of your friends seems "off," ask if everything is all right and see what happens. Just being there to listen—not even to offer a solution but to really just sit and listen without checking your phone or looking around to see if your other friends are nearby—is an incredibly kind and meaningful act.

YOUR TURN

Do you have trouble listening without being distracted? Think about the last time you spoke with a friend when they needed someone to listen to them. How well did you listen? Rate it on a scale of one to ten:

1 2 3 4 5 6 7 8 9 10

EXTREMELY DISTRACTED   (Circle your answer)   FULL ATTENTION

If you find yourself struggling to stay focused, create a list of three to five things that pull your attention away during a conversation—whether it's Instagram, texts, your own thoughts, etc. Then, next to each item, draw an arrow to the right and write down ways you'll ignore these distractions and become a better listener to your friends in the future.

Things that distract me

Ways to ignore them

◆◆◆ **AFFIRMATION** ◆◆◆

In order to hear, I must listen. Listening is the way to
understanding and will help me on the path to true friendship.

Avoid Lapsing Into Bad Friend Behavior

Everyone is capable of slipping into "bad friend" territory by accident—all it takes is a hectic sports schedule or a stressful class for you to morph from friend of the millennium to someone who seems to only care about yourself. The key is being mindful of your friends' needs, not just your own. Think of a time that someone acted like a bad friend. Did she drone on about her own accomplishments and never ask what you had going on? Did he seek a ton of validation or attention from you with no intention of giving back? This behavior is definitely annoying, but keep in mind that you probably do it yourself once in a while.

YOUR TURN

Take a moment and think about a time when someone could have been a better friend (or a time when you could have been a better friend). What kind of behavior did they show that made you uneasy? Inside the blank circles, write some of the behaviors you didn't like.

Now in the hearts, write some behaviors that would have been more helpful or kind. Take a moment to feel gratitude as you write each positive quality. Vow to recognize friends who show that behavior, and do your best to show it as well.

Show Compassion

There's an old Sanskrit word, *maitrī*, which loosely translates to "loving-kindness" or "unconditional friendliness." It could mean unconditional friendliness toward yourself (more on that in the Self-Esteem and Self-Care chapter), but the idea can also be applied to friendliness toward those around you and wishing them well in their own lives. Being compassionate can have a lot of meanings, but it generally refers to showing care and concern for someone. For example, it could be calling a friend whose grandparent is ill, or simply thinking of a friend who's going through a tough time and feeling warmth and concern for him or her. Sending good vibes to people while you meditate is a great way to keep positive energy around them—and you.

YOUR TURN

Take a deep breath in, and let a deep breath out. Take a moment to visualize a friend who is going through a tough time right now. Who comes to mind? Write down their name and draw a quick sketch (or stick figure!) of your friend.

Next, grab a brightly colored pen, pencil, or marker and draw beaming lights shining around your friend and add any symbols or words to represent the good vibes you'd like to send their way. When you're finished, take some mindful deep breaths and visualize yourself sending this positive energy to your friend each time you exhale.

Draw your friend with good vibes around them.

(Write name here)

Work Through a Fight with Your Best Friend

If you're at the beach for a week, odds are there will probably be some beautiful, sunny days but also a rainy day or two. Friendships are kind of like that—you'll deal with your fair share of storms, and, from time to time, you and your BFF will fight. Maybe over an incident at school, maybe over a crush.

But don't worry! This happens in all good friendships, and there's a way to reduce the number of times it happens. In a recent study, psychologists from Wilfrid Laurier University found that friends who knew each other's "triggers," or things that set them off, were less likely to fight. So, if you know your friend freaks out when you don't return the clothes you borrow in a timely manner, you can avoid a fight by returning her stuff right after you use it. Some arguments are likely inevitable, but you can keep them few and far between by thinking of your friend's triggers, communicating clearly what yours are, and, above all, keeping your cool. All storms eventually blow over.

YOUR TURN

If you've had a fight with one of your friends, think about how it started and how you handled it. In each lightning bolt, write a trigger of yours or your friend's that may have sparked the fight.

At the bottom of the scene, draw you and your friend side by side holding a very large umbrella to protect you from the storm. In the umbrella, write "I am cool, calm, and in control." The next time you start arguing with someone close to you, recite this affirmation while taking deep breaths.

(Write trigger here)

Cope with Growing Apart from an Old Friend

Not all friendships stand the test of time. It's perfectly natural for you and your besties from elementary school to grow apart as you get older. They may end up liking video games and computers while you become more interested in theater. That's okay—pursuing different interests doesn't make any of you bad people! Still, it's nice to treat your old BFFs with kindness and not punish them for wanting to pursue other things or make other friends, even though you may feel like you've been abandoned if they move on before you do. It's powerful to simply feel grateful for a friendship that was a key part of a certain phase of your life.

YOUR TURN

A happy way to remember an old friendship is by taking a trip down memory lane. In the space provided, jot down some of your favorite memories with this person. If you decide to reconnect with this friend (see the next entry), you can use these memories as a way to look back at some of the great times you shared together and inspire ideas for future memories to create! If not, just keep it for yourself as a way to get closure, to quietly say goodbye, and to look back on in the future if needed.

MEMORY LANE

MEMORIES WITH

(Old friend's name)

Reconnect with an Old Friend

People grow apart for all sorts of reasons. The great thing is, it's never too late to reconnect with a friend, and odds are that he or she has thought about you just as much but didn't know how to take the first step. Try dropping a line on social media or shooting an email to an old friend, making sure to include a mention of one of your fond memories together. Even though you're not close now, you probably still have some things in common, and those are good topics to bring up. Old friendships can definitely be worth pursuing, making you glad you put in the time.

YOUR TURN

Writing an old friend a letter can help you reconnect. Focus on the love and gratitude you have for the experiences you shared together and positivity toward their future. Suggest a way for your friendship to continue in the present day.

Dear _____,

From,

Survive a Situation When Your Friends Gang Up on You

It happens to everyone at one point or another: Your friends gang up on you. Since your friends are your biggest support system, this situation is really stressful! There's no one answer for how to solve a problem like this, but be sure you're taking care of yourself mentally and physically first and foremost. Talking to your friends calmly can help clear up any misunderstandings. Remember, try not to let your anger, jealousy, or hurt get in the way of a potential solution. Also, don't hesitate to reach out to family members or other trusted people in your life who can help.

YOUR TURN

If you're feeling alone, you might need to be your own support system for a while. In the left-hand column of this chart, list all the ways people usually support you. This can include offering advice, listening to you vent, etc. In the right-hand column, write how you can give yourself a version of that support. For example, if you normally talk to these friends to vent, try journaling how you're feeling to vent your feelings on paper. The next time you meditate or take quiet time for yourself, read your answers, then take deep breaths and repeat an affirmation like "I have all the help and support I need" to help you feel more comfortable and confident in your own abilities throughout this stressful experience.

SUPPORT FROM OTHERS	SUPPORT I CAN OFFER MYSELF

AFFIRMATION

I am calm and in control and will use love when seeking understanding.

Deal with Loneliness and Feeling Left Out

Even when you're surrounded by classmates, teammates, and family, you can still feel lonely and alone. Combine that with advertisements and Instagram feeds showing people having endless hours of fun with their seemingly perfect friends, and it's hard not to feel like everyone except you is having the time of their lives. But the truth is, almost everyone feels left out at one point or another. It's human nature to want to belong, but everyone deals with periods of feeling excluded and lonesome. Remember that bouts of loneliness don't represent your full reality and that you're in charge of how you feel.

YOUR TURN

Social media can make you feel like you're missing out. The truth? You never see the full story behind the photos and videos posted on Instagram and Facebook. Someone posting a fun photo of themselves in a pool with their friends could have an argument with them later that day. Is there anyone you follow online that makes you feel left out? In this rough Instagram profile, write down in the photo grid how their photos make you feel.

Now think about your own social media profile. How might others feel about what *you* post online? What type of image or lifestyle are you sharing with the world and how are you wanting them to perceive you? The next time you're scrolling or posting on social media, brainstorm some ways you can be more mindful of the content you're consuming or sharing with others to help both you and your community feel less alone.

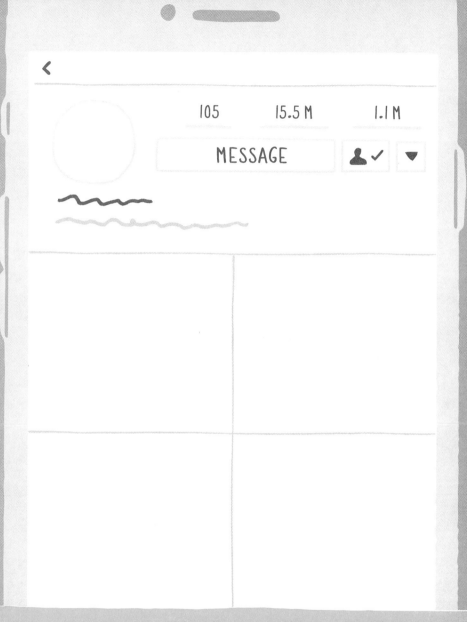

MESSAGE

105   15.5 M   1.1 M

∙◆∙ **AFFIRMATION** ∙◆∙

Loneliness is just a feeling, like any other. When I look inside myself,
I find happiness and fulfillment, light and joy. I use these feelings to
fill myself with happiness, driving away my loneliness.

Travel with Friends
While Still Having Fun

Going on vacation with friends is so exciting—you're off to see the world! You'll also likely be sharing very close quarters with your friend or friends for long stretches of time if you're traveling by plane, train, or car. In fact, a lot of traveling is actually pretty exhausting and stressful, from time spent in transit to decisions about what to do when you arrive at your destination. Lost luggage? Stressful. Money issues? Stress to the max. A clingy friend? Not exactly a walk on the beach. Try to take each experience as it comes and find silver linings along the way. Sometimes the best part of a trip can be a misadventure you and your friend have! Another thing to keep in mind: Just because you're on vacation together doesn't mean you have to be attached at the hip. Find some space and alone time if you need to and it's safe to do so.

YOUR TURN

Stress can be a sneaky stowaway during your fun trip. The trick? Roll with the punches. What are some common misadventures you've experienced while traveling with friends? How did you deal with them? How were you feeling? Is there a way you could have handled these experiences better? Write or draw each scene, then add the emotions you were feeling at the time around each of them. Finally, think of ways you could handle similar misadventures in the future if they occur.

HOW THIS EXPERIENCE FELT

_____
_____
_____

WHAT I'D DO DIFFERENTLY

_____
_____
_____
_____

HOW THIS EXPERIENCE FELT

_____
_____
_____

WHAT I'D DO DIFFERENTLY

_____
_____
_____
_____

◆ ◆ ◆ AFFIRMATION ◆ ◆ ◆

I'm lucky to be able to share a new place with a good friend. I will keep my heart and mind open to new experiences, whatever they may be.

Navigate the Popularity Trap

As long as there have been schools, there have been popular kids—and they always seem to be cooler, thinner, more beautiful, and more interesting than you'll ever be. But here's a secret: These students are just as insecure as you are and in need of just as much reassurance that they're loved and accepted. However, they sometimes have less-than-great ways of showing it. They might make fun of your clothes or your hair or say mean things about you on social media. Or they might not pay you any attention at all. The trick to dealing with not-so-nice popular kids is to realize that not everyone in the world is going to like you (even though you're probably very likable!) and that it's usually a waste of time trying to win their affection. Instead, focus on being positive and maintaining your own meaningful friendships. Realize that other classmates are likely feeling the same way you are, and remember that being popular is transient, but being a good friend is long-lasting.

YOUR TURN

Who are the friends you trust and love most? In the space provided, write their names in fun or interesting fonts. Now think about your individual friendships within the group. Which of these friends help you feel special and loved? Use the following prompt to practice gratitude toward these special friends and show how they prove you don't need to be "popular."

FRIENDS I TRUST AND LOVE MOST

(Write names here)

Being popular isn't important, because I have friends like
_____ (*NAME*). This wonderful friend helps
me feel _____
_____ (*POSITIVE EMOTIONS*) when we hang out together.
_____ (*NAME*) is always _____
_____
_____ (*POSITIVE QUALITIES THEY BRING TO YOU*).

Being popular isn't important, because I have friends like
_____ (*NAME*). This wonderful friend helps
me feel _____
_____ (*POSITIVE EMOTIONS*) when we hang out together.
_____ (*NAME*) is always _____
_____
_____ (*POSITIVE QUALITIES THEY BRING TO YOU*).

◆ ◆ ◆ AFFIRMATION ◆ ◆ ◆

Worrying about how other people perceive me is a poor use of my time.
I will focus my time and energy on enjoying my friendships.

Love Completely

Think about how you use the word "love." Did you "love" that new tie-dye romper you saw on TikTok or that new song by your favorite singer? To love completely is a different level of love, though. It means putting your pride on hold and opening yourself up, making yourself vulnerable (which is a totally scary yet invigorating idea!). Loving someone completely—a friend or parent, for example—requires you to be fully present for another person, accepting that person's flaws, quirks, and, yes, even his or her smelly feet. And this type of love doesn't have to be romantic at all—it can be as simple as being there for a friend in need, showing your parents you love and appreciate them, or allowing yourself to be loved in return.

YOUR TURN

Friendships, romantic relationships, and family all require different types of love. Fill each of these hearts with different ways you express and share your love to the most important people in your life. For example, you may show your love to your family by making dinner for them. Maybe you provide a safe space for your friend to vent when she's feeling angry. Love takes many forms, and there's no one right way to express it!

FRIENDS

FAMILY

BF/GF/
PARTNER

◆ ◆ **AFFIRMATION** ◆ ◆

*When I allow myself to love completely, I open myself up to new
experiences and, in return, open myself up to being loved.*

35

Be Present During Dates

Whether you've asked someone out or been asked out yourself, a date is a super exciting thing. But in between the movie and the macchiato, don't forget why the date is happening in the first place—you and the other person are exploring a connection, so the date is really about learning more about each other. Having a meaningful discussion is hard enough without either of you scrolling through TikTok, Instagram, or Snapchat every other minute, so, as hard as it may be to do, put your phone away. Learn to be present and enjoy the ambiance of a coffee shop or restaurant. Take in the music, the feel of the sofa, the sound of your date's voice, and listen to what they have to say. The first step toward a real connection is making sure a connection actually happens.

YOUR TURN

What are some ways you can be more present and available for your date when you're spending time together? Create a NOT To-Do List of all the distractions you'll try your best to avoid during your date. If you're having trouble thinking of distractions, think about the date itself, then ask yourself what you'll want your date to avoid while you're together. Would it bother you if your date was checking Instagram or Snapchat, for instance?

NOT TO-DO *List*

_____

_____

_____

_____

_____

_____

_____

_____

_____

Right before your date, write down the following affirmation until you feel it resonate within you, and quietly repeat it when you find yourself wanting to reach for your phone or pull away from the moment.

" I am always mindful and in the present."

Actually Have Fun on Your Date!

It goes without saying that dates should be fun—otherwise, what's the point? Don't get hung up on analyzing everything your date does and worrying that they may be having a bad time. Try letting go of expectations and just enjoy your date's company. It's not a job interview or some sort of test; it's a way to get to know someone else. Take your nervous energy and channel it into something productive—like a thoughtful question about the person's interests or an idea for a second date!

YOUR TURN

One way you can have fun and build a connection with your date is by asking them questions and getting to know their interests and dreams. What do you want to learn about your date? Write a list of questions to ask them. After your date, come back to this page and write down what you learned. If the date went well, take a moment to take a few deep breaths and express gratitude for having a fun and meaningful time together. If not, reflect on what you learned from your experience!

QUESTIONS TO ASK YOUR DATE

1 _____

2 _____

3 _____

_____

4 _____

_____

5 _____

_____

6 _____

_____

7 _____

_____

8 _____

_____

9 _____

_____

Heal from a Broken Heart

As much as you hope your relationship will last forever (or at least for the foreseeable future), things happen. Dating in middle school and high school is an imperfect art. Think of how bad you were at spelling when you started kindergarten and how much better you are at it now. It's the same with relationships. With age and time, you'll simply get better at them—including dealing with heartbreak. Whether or not things ended on good terms, keep in mind that as much as things hurt now, the pain will fade in time. Focus on the good parts of your relationship and how you helped each other grow. It's not easy, but reflecting—and eventually moving on—will help you grow.

YOUR TURN

On the next page, label the petals with ways you've grown thanks to this relationship. Have you gained more confidence? Did you learn how to communicate better with a significant other? Did you discover a new hobby or interest you enjoy? Next, think about some qualities you want in a future partner, knowing what you know now. What do you want to avoid? How will you approach your next relationship differently? Write your answers in the clouds.

♦ ♦ ♦ AFFIRMATION ♦ ♦ ♦

Heartache, though painful, can help me grow as a person. I will explore how I feel and remember that, with time, the pain will pass.

Be Mindful of Your Single Friends

It's really difficult when a friend starts dating someone new and exciting. You feel like an afterthought because suddenly your friend and confidante is nothing more than a casual acquaintance who seems to only have time for their new partner.

Now think about how you should act if you're on the other side of things and *you've* just started going out with someone new. Imagine how your friends feel now that you're not spending as much time together. Maybe they're lonely. Maybe they feel resentful of this new person who disrupted your chill group dynamic. Be mindful of their feelings and make an effort to keep your friendships going strong by keeping them in the loop, inviting them to group activities (there's nothing worse than hearing "We didn't think you'd want to come because it was just couples"), and planning some all-important bonding time *without* your new flame.

YOUR TURN ✏

If you're the one in the new relationship, be mindful of your friends' feelings during this shift in the group's dynamic. Write the names of your friends in the left-hand column. Next to each name, write their favorite activities. What are some of your favorite things to do together? Do they have a movie they're interested in seeing? Do you have a favorite lunch spot you go to together every Saturday? Keep these traditions and special activities you share together alive and strong. Look back at this list to check in with yourself to make sure you're still giving your friendships the attention and care they deserve.

NAME	FAVORITE ACTIVITIES

Appreciate the Good Relationships in Your Life

Throughout the day, it's easy to get caught up in whatever's going on. A geometry test. A pop quiz in history. But, in the midst of the chaos, you probably have a constant stream of positive people in your life. Your relationships—whether romantic or platonic—are some of the most important things in your life outside of your family. Remind yourself to take time out of your day to reflect on these people and what they mean to you. Couldn't get through the day without texting one of your friends? Let him know. Love spending time with another friend studying for Spanish exams? Tell her! (En español, if you can.) Find one of your teachers really inspiring? Send them an email saying why. Mindfulness is as much about being conscious of the here and now as it is reflecting on the important things in your life. So why not take that one step further and tell these superstars how much they mean to you? It'll brighten their day and make you that much more thankful.

YOUR TURN

In each phone, write out a sweet text message you can send to a friend, family member, or romantic partner to express your gratitude and love for them. Not sure where to start? Try something like this: "Hi _____ [NAME]! Thank you for being a great friend/loved one/partner in my life. I appreciate you always being _____ [ADJECTIVE] and _____ [ADJECTIVE]. You're the best!"

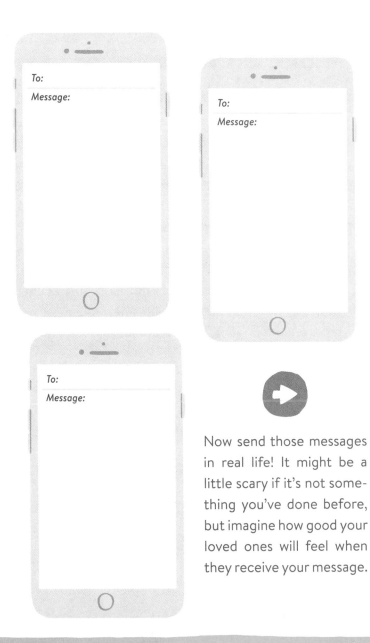

To:

Message:

To:

Message:

To:

Message:

Now send those messages in real life! It might be a little scary if it's not something you've done before, but imagine how good your loved ones will feel when they receive your message.

Move On If They Don't Like You Back

Odds are you've read a poem or heard a song describing the agony of loving someone who doesn't love you back. There's no way around it—loving someone who doesn't feel the same way about you is the worst. But it's not the end of the world. Just because someone doesn't like you back doesn't mean you're not worthy of being liked (or loved). The best thing you can do is realize that there are a number of factors at play—maybe they like someone else, maybe they have no idea you actually like them—and move on. That could mean hanging out more with friends, picking up a new hobby, or working on a self-improvement project (like meditation!).

YOUR TURN

Fill in the following prompt three times and meditate on your answers, especially on days when you're feeling unworthy.

I am worthy of being loved because

I am worthy of being loved because

I am worthy of being loved because

If you're having trouble moving on from this person, brainstorm some mindful activities you enjoy to help you focus on something else.

MINDFUL ACTIVITIES

_____
_____
_____
_____
_____
_____
_____
_____
_____
_____
_____
_____
_____
_____

◆ ◆ AFFIRMATION ◆ ◆

*Just because someone doesn't love me doesn't mean I'm unlovable.
I am an interesting, engaging person worthy of a love that
will find me when the time is right.*

Figure Out Who You Really Like

When you're in your teens, your brain is constantly changing and growing. Think of it like a really complicated city being built one spiraling skyscraper at a time. There's a lot going on, and one experience influences the next. One day, you might like someone in the popular crowd; the next, a brooding artist. That's great—don't hesitate to take this time to figure out who you are as a person and what type of person you like. Think of people you could see yourself getting along with. Who makes you laugh? Who's fun to be around? Don't focus just on looks—there's so much more to a person.

YOUR TURN

As you think about who you might match well with, the most important part to be mindful of is finding someone with similar values. But have you ever thought about what you value? Take some time now to list some beliefs you hold close to your heart.

MY VALUES

Now think about the people in your life. Is there anyone you might be interested in pursuing a relationship with who lives by any of these values? Write down their names and match them with the values on your list. If you're unsure of their values, that's a great opportunity to learn more about the person the next time you talk to each other!

NAME	THEIR VALUES

Accept Others

It's so important to accept others as they are. Everyone deserves to be loved and respected, whether they look different than you, come from a different cultural background or religion, are at a different economic level, or love different people than you do. It's a basic human principle, and the sooner you learn it, the better off you'll be. Approach differences with friendly curiosity, not judgment, sarcasm, or taunting and bullying. Bullies are afraid of things they don't understand and make other people feel bad about things they can't change. The more you try to understand where other people are coming from, the better your life will be. And remember: Before you can be accepting of others, you need to truly accept yourself.

YOUR TURN

One of the best ways to understand and accept others who are different from you is to educate yourself. List some books, documentaries, or podcasts that are focused on topics that highlight other cultures, orientations, backgrounds, etc. Make a list of them here.

HOW I'LL EDUCATE MYSELF

HOW I'LL EDUCATE MYSELF (CONTINUED)

_____
_____
_____
_____

After reading, watching, or listening to these resources, jot down a few lessons you've learned. Think about how you can take what you've learned and apply it to spreading love and acceptance to others in your life.

LESSONS LEARNED

_____
_____
_____
_____
_____
_____
_____
_____

◆ ◆ AFFIRMATION ◆ ◆

Understanding others is key to accepting others—and myself.

Know Your Worth

You're in control of your feelings, no one else. You are very, very worthy and valued, which is a pretty powerful thought. The realization that you have total control over your feelings is comforting in many situations. And no one—not the person you're dating, not a family member, not a teacher—can take that away from you. As bestselling author and psychologist Brené Brown once said, "When you get to a place where you understand that love and belonging, your worthiness, is a birthright and not something you have to earn, anything is possible."

YOUR TURN

Do you remember any past situations where people were saying not-so-nice things about you? Fill in these speech bubbles with their words.

Now cross out all the speech bubbles in whatever way feels right to you. Color them in so you can't read the words anymore or scribble all over them to let your anger out. When finished, take a moment to breathe out any remaining anger or negativity from thinking about what others have said. Next, create a list of things that make you AWESOME! Reflect on this list. Add to it over time. Remember that you are WORTHY.

THINGS THAT MAKE ME
AWESOME

Show Some Respect

Respecting other people seems like Common Courtesy 101, but it isn't always. And we're not just talking about holding doors or saying "please" and "thank you." Respect for another person means respecting their boundaries. If you're texting your girlfriend and she doesn't immediately respond, keep your cool and respect her space. There are a number of reasons why she may seem MIA: A teacher or parent could have confiscated her phone, she could have forgotten it in study hall, her battery might have died, etc. Respect extends way beyond texting, of course—it's a way of life that helps pass along positive energy. Showing respect is really just another way to be mindful of other people.

YOUR TURN

Who are the most respectful people in your life? Write their names in the spaces provided. Add some of the specific actions these people take to showcase and give respect to you and the people in their lives. Now look at the opportunities for respectful action you've written down and brainstorm three ways you're going to implement this kind of respect in your life this week.

NAME	THEIR RESPECTFUL ACTION(S)

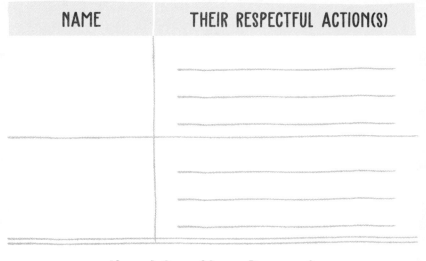

NAME	THEIR RESPECTFUL ACTION(S)

How I Can Show Respect

CHAPTER 2

BRING MINDFULNESS HOME:
Family and Spaces

Families are like branches on a tree.
We grow in different directions but
our roots remain as one.

—Anonymous

You might sometimes find that your family are the last people you want to see or spend time with every day. Whether you have over-bearing parents who won't leave you alone, a sibling who drives you crazy, or a complicated relationship with your family, this area of your life can cause a lot of stress. No matter what your family unit looks like, practicing mindfulness can help you strengthen your relationships with your loved ones and create boundaries that carve out personal space and improve overall mental health.

When you're at home, you need a cherished safe space to help you unwind and relax—especially if you're feeling overwhelmed by family drama, friendships, or schoolwork. Even if you don't have a room of your own, you can still find peace in either your home or one of your favorite places in nature.

This chapter will help you explore mindfulness and personal growth and how you can directly apply these exercises to certain situations with your family and your personal spaces in your home. Some of the topics we'll talk about include:

- Handling overbearing or distant parents
- Managing arguments with your sibling(s)
- Setting boundaries with your family
- Finding peace both indoors and outdoors
- Learning the value of keeping your space organized

Building mindful habits at home will create a solid foundation for tackling other areas of your life that may be causing you stress. After a full day at school filled with exams, projects, and extracurricular activities, the exercises in this chapter can help the experience of coming home become a form of release and peace instead of adding to the stress of your daily life.

Handle Helicopter Parents

Call it what you will—nosy parents, bulldozer parents, or the more popular helicopter parents—these are moms and dads (or other loved ones) who hover over your every move, often doing things that you, as a responsible teenager, could do just as easily (laundry, class projects, buttering your toast, etc.). While these actions usually come from a place of love (yes, your parents want you to succeed!), it can be overwhelming to deal with incessant supervision and fussing. Let them know you appreciate the help but that you need to branch out on your own. However, keep in mind that this freedom works both ways: If you forget your homework or your lunch money, you need to face the music and not have your parents swoop in to save the day.

YOUR TURN

List any situations or activities in your life you'd like to do more on your own, without your parents' or loved one's assistance. For each situation, also write a reason(s) that these particular choices are important to you.

After you've made your list, have a conversation with your loved ones to share your thoughts. You could start with an introduction like "While I do sincerely appreciate you helping me with _____ [RESPONSIBILITY] all these years, it's time for me to handle it on my own. I know you help me out of love, but this is important to me because _____."

SITUATION	REASON

◆◆ AFFIRMATION ◆◆

*My parents want what's best for me and my future. Using that support
and my own independence, I'll propel myself to greatness.*

59

Ask for More Support
from Your Parents

Some parents are very busy, whether with a really demanding job or the responsibility of taking care of other family members. Either way, they might miss some (or all) of your soccer games, PTA meetings, math competitions, and theater performances. Though this can be disappointing, remember that your parents love you. Still, if you want them to be more involved with your activities, tell them how you feel. Maybe they can try to rearrange a meeting to catch some of the game or have someone record your performance so they can watch it later. Honest communication is key to creating any kind of change.

YOUR TURN

Think about some moments or events in your life that your parents weren't able to experience with you. How did you feel? Were you lonely? Angry? Sad, wishing they could share that exciting moment with you? Express those feelings in the space provided.

You can then communicate with your parents about the topic, sharing as much as you want. It may seem like a scary and challenging task, but it's not impossible. There's a chance they're not fully aware of how you're feeling, and now is the time to tell them! Here's a "script" you can try: "_____ [MOM/DAD], I love you and know you support me and I know you're busy, but lately I've been feeling _____ [EMOTION] because you haven't been able to attend _____ [ACTIVITY/EVENT]. It would mean a lot to me if there was a way you could join me in _____ [ACTIVITY/EVENT] in the future. Is there a way we can work on this together?"

EXPRESS YOUR EMOTIONS

Endure an Unfair Punishment

Some parents are always on high alert for signs of misbehavior or disobedience, especially with teenagers. Sometimes you don't deserve punishment because a) your sister did it and framed you, or b) there was just an honest misunderstanding. Here's an important truth: Your parents aren't perfect. It may seem obvious, but truly accepting that your parents aren't perfect or omniscient will really help you in this situation. And, much like your parents, you're not perfect either! When you make bad choices (like we all do sometimes), you most likely appreciate any forgiveness and understanding your parents express in return. Sure, it might come with a punishment as well, but try to extend a similar understanding to your parents when they make mistakes. Forgiveness and empathy for small mishaps and simply moving on is so much better for your stress levels and overall happiness.

YOUR TURN

Let's break down what happened. What did you do that resulted in you getting in trouble? Do you believe your parents were fair with how they dealt with the situation? Really make an effort to be mindful of the entire scenario. Do you still feel the need to speak up? If so, do so calmly. If you're having trouble calming down, fill in this circle with everything you're feeling right now. Don't hold back, just let it go. When you're done, take some deep breaths. Now try again to see what happened from your parents' point of view.

Try your best to move toward forgiveness. Under your circle of emotions, write down the simple phrase "I forgive you." Meditate on it and feel it in your heart as much as you can.

*Learning to be a forgiving, understanding person is
a pursuit worthy of my time.*

Learn from a Fair Punishment

Sometimes you mess up and have to suffer the consequences. Consequences, though a bummer in the moment, are actually a good thing because they remind you that your privileges—whether having a smartphone or being able to stay out late—are in fact privileges, not rights. Try to think of the time while you're grounded as a prime time for mindfulness, where you focus on what you did wrong, how it potentially hurt other people, how you won't do it again, and how you can make better choices in the future. And just because something was taken away from you (like a computer or your phone) doesn't mean you have to feel bored and resentful. Try discovering a new hobby, like writing your feelings in a journal, drawing, or yoga.

YOUR TURN

List some mindful activities or new hobbies you can start while you're unable to watch TV or hang out with friends. Write and/or doodle some examples, then pick one activity to try today and give it a solid attempt for at least thirty minutes. How did it go? Would this be something you'd want to continue doing once your punishment is over? If not, try something new again! You never know what could turn into a new passion.

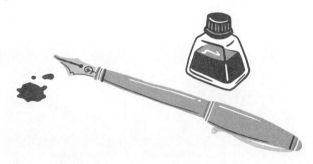

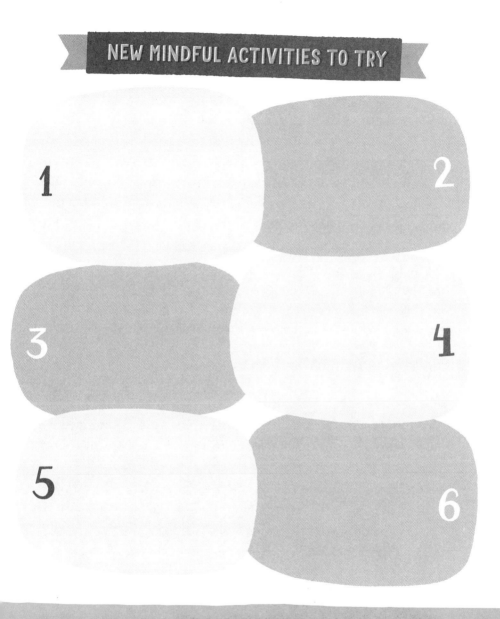

1

2

3

4

5

6

• • AFFIRMATION • •

No one is perfect, and being grounded is a time to reflect on how I can be better.

Stop Fighting with Your Siblings

Sometimes you might feel as though your brothers and sisters were put on this planet solely to annoy you and get you punished, setting traps for you at every turn and waiting for you to screw up. These fights are typically rooted in some form of sibling rivalry. For example, you compete with your siblings for things like attention, space, and privileges. Who gets more time with Mom and Dad? Who gets the bigger bedroom? Who gets to stay up until eleven? Instead of looking at your siblings as rivals, however, think of them as teammates. Each of you has a different role, but you're all working together toward a common goal—a happy home life. Cooperation will work much better than an every-man-for-himself competition in achieving a smoother and more harmonious family life.

YOUR TURN

What are some of your favorite memories with your sibling(s)? Illustrate some of the best moments you've shared together in these photo boxes, then take a moment to reflect on those moments. What made them special? What was it that helped you get along so well? Keep these moments and the reasons why they were special close to your heart the next time you find yourself annoyed by your sibling(s). When you feel negative feelings creeping in, take a breath, smile, and approach them with kindness as much as possible.

◆ ◆ AFFIRMATION ◆ ◆

*There's no one else in the world like a sibling. I will be present when
I'm with mine and learn to ask questions, hear what they have to say,
and realize that differences help us all grow.*

67

Cope with a Growing Family

Families are always changing and growing. Maybe your parents have just told you that you're about to become a big brother or big sister and it's time to get excited about helping to care for a new life, or maybe one of your parents is remarrying and some stepbrothers or stepsisters are entering the equation. Sure, this is a huge change that will take some getting used to, but it can also be exciting and fun. Remember that every moment with your siblings—new, old, step, or half—is precious. There is no cookie-cutter family, no right or wrong size or makeup, so find a way to celebrate that and embrace being part of a truly modern family.

YOUR TURN

You're soon going to have a new sibling—or siblings!—joining your family. How do you feel about this upcoming change? Find some colored pencils, markers, or crayons and pick out the color(s) that best represent how you feel. Use those colors to create a word cloud about your feelings on this big change in your family. Write your strongest feelings in large letters and more neutral or calm emotions in smaller letters. See this quick example for ideas.

nervous happy

fear of the
unknown **excited**

MY FEELINGS ABOUT MY NEW SIBLING(S)

Handle a Move to a New Place

Moves are stressful, no doubt, but they can also be a fun and positive change. You'll likely feel a mixture of complex emotions all at once— excited, scared, sad, nervous, and so on. Be sure to recognize and name your feelings and accept that each one is valid. Once you've officially moved, try to focus on all the things you're thankful for at your new home. Centering your thoughts on the positive will help you deal better with any negative feelings you may have.

YOUR TURN

What are some of the good parts of your new home? Is the weather sunnier and warmer? Are you closer to some family members than you were before? Does your house have more space, or is your apartment close to school? Draw an outline of your new home and fill it with things you're thankful for. Feel free to continue adding to it as you discover more wonderful things about your new spot.

WHAT'S GREAT ABOUT MY NEW HOME

◆ ◆ ◆ **AFFIRMATION** ◆ ◆ ◆

Moving to a different place gives me the opportunity to discover new things. My heart is open, my feet are ready to explore, and my mind is ready to learn.

Deal with Embarrassing Parents

There are going to be times when you and your parents aren't on the same page. Maybe it's their questionable fashion choices, their inability to understand why you really need pink—sorry, rose gold—hair, or the embarrassing way they talk. Whatever the disconnect, try not to focus on it. Your parents are allowed to be clueless about fads, even though it probably makes you squirm when your dad tries to act cool with your friends. Just remember that they're doing this from a place of love, and your mom's fashion sense (or lack thereof) isn't what's important. Your parents' love for you is what matters most. In fact, if you were able to look ten years into the future, you'd realize most kids are in the same boat and that this kind of embarrassment really doesn't matter at all.

YOUR TURN

Take a moment and really think: When your parents want to talk to you and learn more about your life and what kids are into nowadays, do you shrug them off or actually have a conversation and open up to them? Consider which of your interests and passions you could share with them and jot them down.

Now it's time to show some gratitude! Draw your parents in the empty space. Include their favorite outfits and any unique features that make them special. Then, in either a list format or by adding to the drawing, include everything you love about your parents. Remember these special qualities the next time you feel like rolling your eyes after your dad tries to say something "hip" or your mom does something embarrassing in front of your friends.

INTERESTS I COULD SHARE WITH MY PARENTS

_____   _____

_____   _____

_____   _____

Request More Boundaries from Your Parents

Maybe it started early. You'd go to the grocery store with your parents as a young child and see a sweet cereal you absolutely had to have. You begged, pleaded, goaded—and got what you wanted. But small treats when you were a kid led to bigger leniencies and concessions. Curfew? Nope, you can stay out as late as you want.

Getting everything you want all the time—or having parents who don't set boundaries—seems like a teenager's dream, but it's an illusion. That nagging and pestering and checking in exists for a reason: to help you learn what's right and wrong and how to make good decisions. If you yearn for more rules, it never hurts to ask for them or to tell your parents how you're feeling. If they're not up for it, set your own boundaries.

YOUR TURN

If you feel like you need more boundaries in your life, think of some areas you feel unsure about or that are negatively affecting you in a way you don't know how to improve. Maybe you feel like you watch too much Netflix or are struggling to study enough for tests. Write down one of these aspects of your life in the center of the square.

If you've talked to your parents and still aren't getting what you need from them, make your own boundaries. On the sides of the square, write small steps you can take to start creating boundaries for yourself. Choose one of these baby steps to try this week. After you feel like you've formed a habit, try another baby step, then another. Habits take time to develop, so be patient with yourself.

Creating Healthy Boundaries

•♦• AFFIRMATION •♦•

Structure exists to make my life more balanced.
Creating boundaries is a way to help me achieve my goals.

Declutter Your Space

It's funny to think about how much stuff we accumulate over time: shoes, clothes, games, electronic devices, books (well, sometimes), class notes, sports equipment, souvenirs, birthday cards and presents from your family (including that itchy sweater you're forced to wear at Christmas). The list goes on and on. Your stuff is an extension of who you are, and there's a huge amount of comfort in being surrounded by it. But stuff doesn't define who you are. When you're looking at a room full of clutter, you're looking at total chaos!

Marie Kondo, author of *The Life-Changing Magic of Tidying Up*, has a simple yet genius solution—ask yourself if a particular item gives you joy. If not, get rid of it (or donate it!). You'll find you really don't need all the stuff you think you do, and your mind will thank you for the extra space.

YOUR TURN

Find an area in your room that has clutter. This could be your desk, your closet, under your bed, etc. Pick one area to focus on first.

Take a good look at everything in that space. Write down how it makes you feel. Are you overwhelmed? Stressed? Annoyed? Calm? Now use that awareness when you go through your items to see what you want to keep, donate, or get rid of completely. Once you've decluttered, look at that space again. What feelings come up now? Jot them down and note what changed from Before to After.

FEELINGS ABOUT MY SPACE

BEFORE DECLUTTERING	AFTER DECLUTTERING

◆◆ AFFIRMATION ◆◆

Objects in my life should bring me joy.
A cluttered space leads to a cluttered mind.

Do Some Chores!

Let's be real: Chores aren't usually very fun. Those dirty pots and pans taunt you from miles away, reminding you that you can't really relax until they're sitting spick-and-span in the cabinets. But studies have shown that doing chores—especially starting to do them at an early age—is good for everyone in the house. According to Marty Rossmann, professor emeritus at the University of Minnesota, kids who were given chores early in life—around four years old—had a more solid relationship with their parents. But wait, there's more! These floor-sweeping, lawn-mowing helpers were also found to be more self-sufficient and had better grades. So rather than thinking of chores as, well, a chore, think of them as the ultimate exercise in mindfulness. Use that time to reflect and meditate, and maybe, just maybe, your chores won't seem so daunting.

YOUR TURN

What's one chore you absolutely can't stand? What is it about that chore that makes you feel this way? Is there any way you can make this chore not feel so annoying? Are you able to listen to your favorite music or a new podcast as you do it? Write down some ideas. Another way to help yourself feel less annoyed about having to do chores is to give yourself a reward afterward, such as watching your favorite show or playing your favorite video game. What are three ways you can reward yourself for completing your chores?

HOW TO MAKE MY CHORES LESS BORING

_____

_____

_____

_____

_____

THREE WAYS TO REWARD MYSELF

1 _____

2 _____

3 _____

◆ ◆ ◆ AFFIRMATION ◆ ◆ ◆

Chores and cleaning are just another way for me to practice mindfulness.
The time spent doing them is sacred time, carved out just for me.
It is my time, and I will use it fully.

Help Out Around the House (No, Really!)

Chores are one thing, but proactively helping around the house kicks your contributions to the household up a notch. Think of chores as homework that is expected of you no matter what and additional help around the house as extra credit that will earn you major points with your parents. It goes beyond doing laundry and taking out the trash into the territory of being the greatest kid your parents could ever ask for. How can you help around the house? Anticipate needs. If you use the end of the toilet paper roll, replace it. If it's not your turn to do laundry but you see a big load of sheets that needs washing, wash and fold away. You'll be doing your parents a favor, and, as an added bonus, being proactive often has the benefit of getting your mom and dad to ease up on being helicopter parents and micromanaging. Only good things will come of proving you're responsible and thoughtful.

YOUR TURN

Take some time to think about all the things your parents do for you, such as going grocery shopping, making dinner every night, packing your lunch, driving you to school, etc. Make a list of these tasks, then take a moment to really feel gratitude for what they do for you. Now circle at least one of these things that you can start doing on your own.

THINGS MY PARENTS DO FOR ME

Clean Your Room

Picture this: You're up at 5 a.m. for swim practice and have to head straight from school to a swim meet, followed by a study group for your upcoming math test. And you have a book report due tomorrow. In the midst of all of this, it's easy to forget that your bedroom chair isn't actually your closet, your towel shouldn't live on the floor, and the kitchen counter isn't a landing spot for unwashed dishes. But something has to give, doesn't it? Not necessarily. Try waking up just ten or fifteen minutes earlier (ugh, I know!) to pay some attention to your room—quickly put away your socks, hang up your clothes and towels, and bring your dirty glasses to the dishwasher. While it may be painful to hear the alarm so early, remember that the peace you'll find in coming home to a neat room is worth it (especially when you can actually find your socks).

YOUR TURN

The next time you clean your room, time yourself. How long does it take? Write down that number in the timer. Knowing how long it takes to clean your room, how much earlier would you need to get up in the morning in order to tidy up before starting your day? If morning isn't your best time, when else could you find this time during the day? Jot down three ideas.

TIME IT TOOK TO
CLEAN MY ROOM

TIMES I COULD CLEAN MY ROOM

1 _____
_____

2 _____
_____

3 _____
_____

Create a Chill Spot in Your Room

Your room is probably where you spend a lot of your time when you're home. You sleep there, your clothes are there (hopefully in closets or drawers and not on the floor), and the rest of your stuff is there too. You probably use your room as a space to do homework or hang out with friends. Consider making it a spot to practice mindfulness too. Pick a corner of your room you can use as a place to meditate and feel calm. It should be away from electronics like your TV or computer and any other potential distractions. Use your time in your meditation spot to center yourself and breathe and to feel totally cool, calm, and collected.

YOUR TURN

Imagine the perfect chill corner in your room. What does it look like? How does it make you feel? It doesn't have to be anything dramatic, maybe just a cute rug or floor pillow. Describe or draw what this looks like. Now brainstorm some mindful activities you'll do in this new space. Will you meditate, read, listen to podcasts, or something else? Add your ideas to your Peaceful To-Do List.

Peaceful **TO-DO** *List*

_____   _____

_____   _____

_____   _____

◆ ◆ ◆ AFFIRMATION ◆ ◆

*My space is my own, and surrounding myself with
calm tranquility leads to a peaceful mind.*

Appreciate the Great Outdoors

When was the last time you stopped to observe a beautiful tree or smell the roses? Your only contact with nature shouldn't be the ocean-scented hand soap in your bathroom. Give yourself time to go outside as much as you can, and enjoy being out there. Bring a book to read, write in a journal, or just hang out with a friend in your back-yard. Even if you live in a big city, there are plenty of parks where you can appreciate flowers and trees. Make sure to focus on the sound of the wind rustling the leaves, the way the sun dances through the tree canopy, and the birdsong around you. It's more restorative than you might think and a great way to calm an overburdened mind.

YOUR TURN

What are some of your favorite places to visit in nature? Do you prefer the beach or the woods? Maybe a grassy park with flowers? Grab some colored pencils and draw your ideal nature scene. Is there anywhere in your neighborhood or city you can visit that's similar to this? If you prefer the beach but don't live anywhere near one, is there a different body of water you can visit to help connect your-self with nature?

MY FAVORITE SPOTS IN NATURE

◆◆◆ **AFFIRMATION** ◆◆◆

Pursuing serene moments in nature,
I take in the beauty and calmness around me.

CHAPTER 3

KEEP CALM AND STUDY ON:
School

*One child, one teacher, one pen,
and one book can change the world.*

—Malala Yousafzai, Nobel Peace Prize–winner
and education advocate

Most students have a love/hate relationship with school. School is the place where you spend most of your life, which can be frustrating, but also really fun! While you're in school, you get to spend time with some of your favorite people, play your favorite sports, (hopefully) run into your crush, and learn some new things. However, you also have to deal with the stressful side of school, which can include strict teachers, seemingly endless amounts of homework, tough tests, huge long-term research projects, early morning practices, late nights studying, and dealing with choosing and trying to get accepted into your dream college. That's a lot to deal with at once!

One of the best ways you can handle both the good and not-so-good parts of school is by practicing mindfulness and self-care. This chapter will help you through some of the biggest challenges you can experience in school and show you how mindfulness can help you cope with them. Some scenarios you'll tackle in this chapter include:

- Staying focused while studying for exams
- Effectively managing your time
- Handling failure
- Navigating college applications
- Bringing mindfulness into your hobbies, such as sports and music
- And so much more

School takes up so much of your time; why not make it easier to manage and a more positive experience? In this chapter, you'll learn how to be less distracted by social media while doing homework or studying, deal with failure and rejections from colleges with ease, and feel more comfortable with not knowing what the future holds. Let's get started!

Start a New School

Picture this: One of your parents gets a new job in a different state, meaning you have to move and enroll in a new school, leaving behind your old classmates, friends, and teachers. Stepping through the doors for the first time is incredibly nerve-wracking, and you're probably angry at your parents for uprooting you from a familiar place. Instead of fuming at them, try to see your new school in a positive light. For example, maybe this school has some fun extracurricular activities your old one didn't or better class options. Keep yourself open to new possibilities and friendships, and you'll stay on the path to success.

YOUR TURN

Having trouble adjusting to your new school and appreciating the positives? Try the ideas on the following checklist, filled with activities and tasks that have been crafted to help you have a great start to your new school experience.

HOW I CAN MAKE THE MOST
of MY NEW SCHOOL

- Explore your new school before your first day! Ask if someone on the school staff can give you a tour or if you and your family can have permission to explore on your own.

- Ask to introduce yourself to your teacher(s) ahead of time.

- Get to know your guidance counselor or any assisting school staff members that can be a resource for helping you navigate any areas you might need help with.

- Attend any events before or early in the school year so you and your family can meet new people.

- Join at least one club or extracurricular activity.

- Introduce yourself to one person in your class(es). You never know. You might make a new friend!

- Spend one week writing down at least one thing a day about your new school that you're thankful for to help you focus on the positives.

◆◇ AFFIRMATION ◇◆

I am intelligent, capable, and strong and can handle any obstacle put before me.

Commute Mindfully

Getting to and from school every day can be a drag. Maybe your parents drive you, you carpool with some neighbors, or you take the bus or subway. However you travel, you have to do it twice a day, every day of the school year. That's a lot of back and forth—and a lot of opportunities to focus on the here and now! Instead of zoning out or staring at your phone, use that time to focus on how you're feeling. By being present, you help your mind focus and make every single commute new and different.

YOUR TURN

As you commute, think of what you're experiencing. How does your body feel? Tired? Elated? Now think about each of your five senses. Focus on the sounds around you: maybe it's your friends chatting happily behind you on the bus, your big brother singing along to the radio, or the sound of rain hitting the windshield. What do you see? Buildings? Trees? Can you smell anything specific? Are you eating anything tasty?

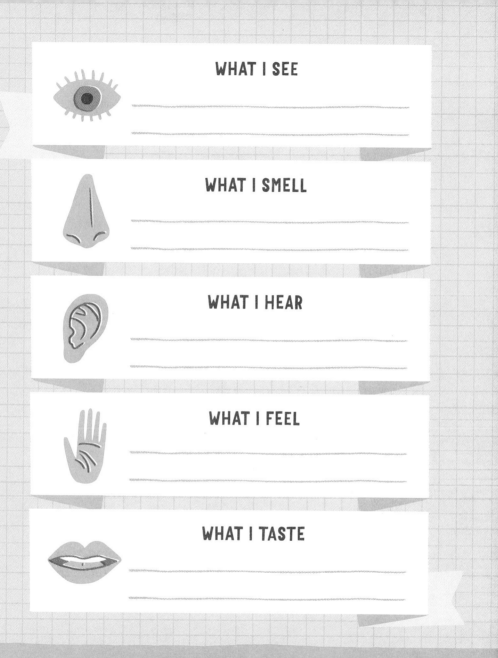

WHAT I SEE

WHAT I SMELL

WHAT I HEAR

WHAT I FEEL

WHAT I TASTE

◆·◆ AFFIRMATION ◆·◆

Using my senses, I see, hear, and feel everything around me.

Pay Attention in Class

At some point, even the most interesting subjects can sound boring and unintelligible as your teacher drones on like a noisy old vacuum cleaner. Unfortunately, you still have to figure out how to pay attention (your grade depends on it, after all!). There are a ton of tips and tricks for doing this. For instance, you can sit in the front row so you're forced to pay attention and can't start daydreaming. Raise your hand often to answer questions and make sure to sit far away from the class clown. Even playing a game where you challenge yourself to take the most detailed notes possible will help since you're competing against the toughest critic you know—yourself.

Don't be too hard on yourself if you do start to lose focus though! Creating good focusing habits takes time. Whenever you notice your attention going elsewhere, mentally acknowledge it, pull your focus back, and kindly tell yourself "I am focused and paying attention to my teacher and what's needed from me for my class."

YOUR TURN

One of the first steps to becoming more focused is noticing your biggest distractions. The next time you're in class, notice what pulls your focus the most. Is it your friends? Your phone? Other students walking by the window? List these in the left-hand column. Now note in the right-hand column all the ways you can avoid these distractions in the future.

DISTRACTIONS	WHAT I CAN DO ABOUT THEM

AFFIRMATION

My attention is my own, and I will call it to my use in and out of class.

Focus On a Long-Term Project

Odds are, at some point in your life, you've been assigned a long-term project like a book report, a presentation, or a term paper that requires days (if not weeks) of research and collaboration with your classmates. While it's tempting to ignore it until the week it's due, that's not a good plan. Being mindful of deadlines is the best way to tackle any large assignment and prevent yourself from becoming panicked or overwhelmed. If you're working on a term paper and have a month to do it, start as soon as you receive the assignment, making an outline, doing research, and keeping track of what parts of the assignment you still have to check off the to-do list. Planning your time well means you'll ultimately have much less stress as your project's due date approaches.

YOUR TURN

Look at how much time you have to complete your big project. What steps do you need to take to complete it? Write down all of them. Being more detailed will help! With all these steps in mind, create a timeline to represent when you're going to complete each one. Following this schedule will help you stay mindful of your time, workload, and progress and will be an important life skill for other big projects in your future!

TASKS TO COMPLETE

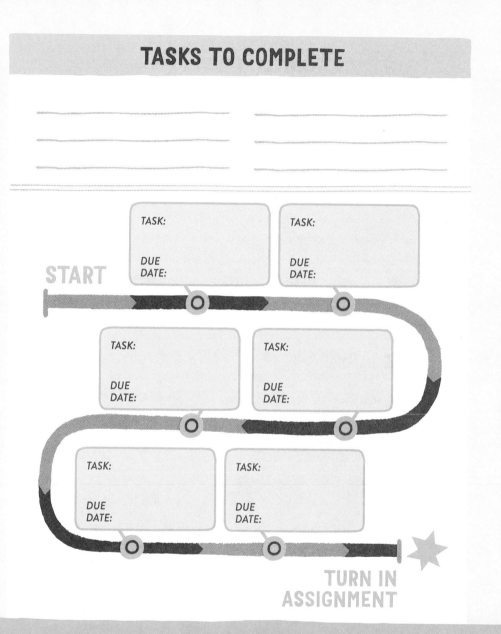

START

TASK:

DUE
DATE:

TASK:

DUE
DATE:

TASK:

DUE
DATE:

TASK:

DUE
DATE:

TASK:

DUE
DATE:

TASK:

DUE
DATE:

TURN IN
ASSIGNMENT

◆ ◆ AFFIRMATION ◆ ◆

*Time only moves forward, so I will make sure to use my time
in such a way that I won't regret looking back.*

Understand Your Teacher

Not all teachers are perfect. In fact, you can probably name at least one teacher you had that you didn't particularly like. Maybe you thought they never liked you or that they assigned some of the hardest projects. While you're going to experience a wide variety of teachers (from amazing to not-so-great), it's important to remember that teachers are human, just like you. And, like you, they have flaws and are trying their best in any given situation. You never know what this teacher may be experiencing outside of the classroom. If you're struggling to make a connection with one of your teachers, try your best to at the very least meet them halfway and consider what they might be experiencing each day.

YOUR TURN

Do you have a teacher in your life you're having a hard time connecting with? What do you think is causing the disconnect between their teaching and you learning in their class? Remember, it might not be about you. Instead of focusing on the negative, think of three good things about this teacher.

Then, try to brainstorm at least one way you can try to better connect with this teacher. If you don't understand a specific lesson, see if you can meet with your teacher outside of class to try to better understand the subject matter. If you were acting out during class, don't be afraid to sincerely apologize for your behavior. Small actions can have a huge impact, even something as simple as an apology.

THREE GOOD THINGS ABOUT THIS TEACHER

1 _____

2 _____

3 _____

IDEAS ON HOW TO CONNECT WITH THIS TEACHER

1 _____

2 _____

3 _____

Master Public Speaking

It's the moment every student dreads—when the teacher calls you to the front of the class to deliver a book report or presentation. Your palms are sweaty, your knees are shaking, and your mouth suddenly feels like cotton. You're terrified you've forgotten all of your talking points, and your mind goes blank. This is a totally natural reaction to a high-stress situation, but that doesn't make it any better. The best thing you can do is practice. Plus, think of it this way—all of your classmates will eventually have to get up and speak, right? They're probably just as nervous as you are. But don't try the age-old trick of picturing the audience in their underwear (trust me, it's just weird); instead, take calm, centering breaths. Look around for familiar faces that can help encourage you as you go. Now draw your shoulders back, straighten your notes, and smile. You're prepared, you're poised, and you've totally got this.

YOUR TURN

On a scale of one to ten, how nervous or scared do you feel about presenting in front of other people?

1 2 3 4 5 6 7 8 9 10

COOL, CALM, AND
COLLECTED
(Circle your answer)
OUT-OF-YOUR-MIND
TERRIFIED

If you're feeling around a five or above, why do you think you're feeling that way? What is it about public speaking that scares you the most? Is there a worst-case scenario rattling around your head?

Write or draw it here. Imagine if your worst-case scenario actually happened (you forget what to say, you say the wrong thing, etc.). How would you truly handle that situation, and what would happen after? (**HINT:** The picture in your head is usually way worse than what happens in real life.)

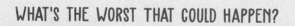

WHAT'S THE WORST THAT COULD HAPPEN?

◆ ◆ ◆ AFFIRMATION ◆ ◆ ◆

*I'm happy to be here, and the knowledge I share
will be useful and interesting.*

Study Instead of Using Snapchat

The draw of social media is—to put it mildly—irresistible. Study after study has shown that the more you use your smartphone, the more you want to use it. One study reported on CNN found that teens who were most active on social media checked their social networks more than one hundred times a day. Clearly it is super hard to put your phone down and be present. When you have a big test to study for, try making some rules. For example, give your phone to a sibling or parent and tell that person not to give it back until you've finished your homework for the night or memorized the material for a big test. Or, if you think you have the willpower, try simply shutting down your phone for a few hours so you're not tempted to check each buzz or ding.

YOUR TURN

One way to be more mindful about how often you use your phone is to have a clear idea of how much you actually use it in the first place (even outside of the time you should be studying). Check your phone's screen use time or download an app that tracks how often you use it. What does it say about an average day? Are you surprised by these numbers? Write down some of your findings.

Then, write a promise to yourself that you'll keep your phone off or away from you for *at least* one hour at a time when you need to focus on schoolwork. For example, you could write "I promise to focus on studying for at least one hour a day during the week without looking at my phone."

SCREEN TIME *Findings*

_____   _____
_____   _____
_____   _____
_____   _____
_____   _____

I promise to focus on _____

_____

(*STUDYING, HOMEWORK, CHORES, ETC.*) for
at least _____
(*TIME FRAME*) a day during the week
without looking at my phone.

_____
SIGN HERE

Prep for Tests

If the acronyms SAT or ACT strike fear into your very being, you dread the upcoming proficiency test, or you've ever stared at a blank exam because you just can't seem to get your brain into gear, don't worry! Tests, like anything else in life, require preparation. You wouldn't compete in a soccer tournament without having practiced all season, and the same is true of test taking. Everyone studies in his or her own way, but to study efficiently you need to find a routine that works best for you—and stick to it! That may mean finding a quiet place in the library to sit and read for a few hours or making sure you have a spot equipped with enough water and snacks so you're not constantly getting up in search of sustenance. Studies have shown that even changing the room you study in can be hugely beneficial for retaining information, so switch it up and prepare to be amazed.

YOUR TURN

What room do you usually study in? Do you find it effective to always study in the same place? If not, switch it up! Where are some other places you can study effectively? Even something small like moving to a different space in your usual room might help. Draw the new area you're going to study in and be mindful and gracious of the peaceful space where you plan to do your schoolwork in the future.

MY IDEAL STUDY ROOM

◆ ◇ ◆ AFFIRMATION ◆ ◇ ◆

By consciously honing my study skills,
I pave the way to success brick by brick.

Study More Effectively

How do you actually hit the books and remember everything you packed into your brain? The key is being mindful of how you learn best. Not everyone learns the same way. Some people learn best by listening, some are more visual, and some need a more hands-on approach to better understand something. If you're studying for a big biology test and you've had trouble memorizing that the mitochondria are the powerhouses of the cell (or anything else for any other exams), try a different method this time. Create flashcards, join a study group, ask a friend to quiz you on the material, or sketch images that help you visualize what you need to learn. Another important thing? Remember to reward yourself with the occasional break so you can give your mind a breather. When it comes time to take your test, take a few deep breaths beforehand and remind yourself that you've got this.

YOUR TURN

Have you tried different ways of studying to see what works best for you? Fill out the following chart (and add your own methods!) to keep track of what types of study methods are most effective by adding a checkmark to the methods that helped and an **X** to the ones that didn't. Each subject may require different methods, and that's okay! What matters is that you're familiar with how you learn best.

WAYS to STUDY

SUBJECT /CLASS	FLASH CARDS	ONLINE QUIZZES	STUDY GROUP	REVIEWING NOTES	PRACTICE QUESTIONS	OTHER
EXAMPLE: SCIENCE	✓		✓	✓		

◆◆ AFFIRMATION ◆◆

Being smart about my studying will also help me be wiser.

Cram for a Test

You've got a big test coming up, and you realize you've spent more time on social media over the past few weeks than you have studying for it. There's no need to panic, though. Instead of mindlessly flipping through the relevant material at the eleventh hour, try refocusing your negative energy on something positive for your mind and body.

Breathe deeply and think about how best to spend the time remaining before the test. Think about productive ways to gather and remember key information. Take time to center yourself and come up with a plan of attack that will leave you ready and refreshed come test day. This could include studying with friends, making time for working out, getting a good night's sleep, or just being mindful about what your brain (and body!) is telling you as you try to remember Darwin's theory of evolution.

YOUR TURN

Think about some exams you aced thanks to effective studying. What are some of the mindful habits you used for those exams? Think of ideas like meditating or getting enough sleep. Refer back to this list when you need a last-minute boost before your test!

EMERGENCY
STUDY KIT

Feel Empowered in Social Situations

Dances, clubs, rallies, lunchtime, group projects...throughout your time in both middle school and high school (and even when you get to college!), school is filled with tons of social situations. While some people thrive in social settings (hello, extroverts!), you may not feel as excited to interact with other people in these situations. Whether you're shy, feel uncomfortable in large groups, have a hard time connecting with new people, or anything else, first know that you are not a bad person for feeling this way. Some people aren't naturally gifted with being able to blossom in social settings, and that's okay! But if a school dance or finding people to sit with at lunch is causing anxiety and stress, try bringing mindfulness and gratitude into these scenarios. Do you have one person you can connect with before the school dance to make sure you arrive together? Did one person in the new club you joined acknowledge your good idea? Small cumulative moments like this can help you appreciate social settings even more and help lessen the anxiety that may have arisen when you first encountered these situations.

YOUR TURN

In the center of the sun, write down one social situation that causes you stress or makes you anxious. On each ray of sunshine, write down at least one positive thing that happened each time you were in this situation. The more you practice this, the more often you'll approach this scenario looking for the good, rather than expecting the worst.

Choose a College the Mindful Way

There's more pressure than ever before on teens to start thinking early about their higher education. The college admissions process is cutthroat, and the competition for scholarships has grown more intense. All of that translates into lots of stress for you: making sure you have the right extracurriculars, impeccable grades, hours of test prep classes and quizzes, and knockout letters of recommendation. Not only is the frenzy unsustainable; it also isn't healthy, since you're setting yourself up to burn out. Instead, focus on the kinds of things you want from a college (specific course choices or good internship opportunities, for instance) and what reasonable things you can do to make yourself a good candidate. Don't worry about what college is at the top of some magazine's ranking—remember that you're trying to find a school that's the best fit for you.

YOUR TURN

Think about your dream college experience. Divide the things you'd like to have into two lists: Must-Haves (you won't go to a school that doesn't offer these, whether it's a specific course of study or a strong financial aid package) and Nice-to-Haves (these things would really make your experience better but you could live without them if necessary, like single dorm rooms). Now that you've envisioned your ideal school, do some research! Use these lists to help you prioritize which schools fit you best. Do any schools have all of your Must-Haves and some of your Nice-to-Haves? Be sure to look into applying there!

MUST-HAVES	NICE-TO-HAVES

◆◆ AFFIRMATION ◆◆

I acknowledge that the journey to college is a long one and will be stressful, but I'll use this pressure to my advantage, constantly reminding myself that I am more than the schools that accept me.

Move On from a College Rejection

Your applications have been submitted and now you're frantically checking your mail (or email) to see if you got into your dream school. Suddenly, there's the letter starting with "Due to the overwhelming number of qualified applicants this year..." —you didn't get in. It's understandable you're disappointed, and it's okay to let yourself be sad, but a rejection letter is not the end of the world.

If this school really was the only place you could ever see yourself, talk to your parents or someone you trust about other options (and there are always other options, even if it doesn't seem like it right now!). Maybe you can take classes at another college and try transferring in the next year, using your good grades and excellent recommendations as proof you're just too good to pass up. The point is, a rejection from your top school isn't a rejection of *you*. And there's probably a whole list of schools that would be delighted to have you.

YOUR TURN

First, let's work through your current emotions after receiving the rejection letter. Grab some colored pencils, crayons, markers, or anything else with color! In the space on the next page, write down anything that represents how you're feeling—words, scribbles, icons, etc. Then list positive things. These can be things you feel will happen from this event, things you believe about yourself, or just five things from your life in general. As you write them down, take deep breaths and repeat the following affirmation: "I am not defined by a school's choice."

POSITIVE THINGS

_____

_____

_____

_____

_____

♦ ♦ AFFIRMATION ♦ ♦

_Instead of obsessing over the things I cannot change,
I will focus my energy on what I did well; just because one college
turned me down doesn't mean I don't have other options._

Balance School Life and Normal Life

School takes up not only a majority of your day but also a majority of your life. You've probably been in school for more than a decade by now—countless hours spent with multiplication tables, textbooks, and science equipment—and while it's a huge part of your life right now, it won't always be. Your close family and friends are the foundation for a good life beyond your school years. Plus, you probably have other groups you're part of that will last beyond school—maybe you're involved with your church, synagogue, or mosque, or you volunteer at a soup kitchen occasionally. Yes, school is important, and doing well there is important too, but you shouldn't put it above being a good family member or friend. Taking stock of the things that are truly important will help you maintain perspective, which is essential for helping you ace not just school but life.

YOUR TURN

Think about your daily life. What do you prioritize? What do you find yourself spending the most time on? Is school your number one? Friends? Sports? List them in order, and be honest with yourself.

Take a look at your list. Are you happy with your priorities? Do you feel like you live a balanced life? Why or why not? If you're not satisfied with your priorities, which one would you like to focus on to help you feel more balanced? Try to do at least one small activity each day to help move this part of your life higher among your priorities.

My CURRENT PRIORITIES

1 _____
2 _____
3 _____
4 _____
5 _____
6 _____
7 _____
8 _____
9 _____
10 _____

FOCUS MORE ON # _____ (NUMBER)

by doing this: _____

_____

_____

♦ ♦ AFFIRMATION ♦ ♦

My life at school is not my whole life.
By taking stock of the other parts of my life and making time for others,
I can more accurately gauge what's important.

Cope with Failing a Test

Sometimes a test gets the better of you. Maybe you didn't under-stand or retain the subject matter (...uh, what is inorganic chemistry again? Which guy was the thirteenth president?), you procrastinated instead of studying, or maybe you even wrote down the wrong test date (hey, it happens!). Whatever the reason, acknowledge it and take responsibility. It's never a good strategy to blame outside influences for your mistakes. Breathe in and realize that one mistake does not define you. Breathe out, calm your mind, and resolve to work not just harder but better. A failed test isn't the end of the world, but it does mean you need to re-evaluate the way you approach the next test. Maybe you can't make up that failed test, but ask yourself how you can better prepare for next time.

YOUR TURN

The process of writing something down can help you remember it. To help yourself focus your attention on something positive, write down this sentence at least ten times (or even more on a separate piece of paper) until you start to believe it yourself: "I am not defined by a failed test; I am smart and successful." As you write, breathe in and out and know that failure isn't the end of the line; it's simply a redirection to teach you how to handle something differently in the future.

I am not defined by a failed test;
I am smart and successful.

Stay Grounded Even in Success

Maybe school comes easy to you and you're the kind of person who can ace a test without cracking open a single book (lucky you!). It's easy to get teachers to like you, and you know even before you get a term paper back that there's going to be a big red "A" on top of it. First off, it's great that you're doing well! Succeeding—whether it comes through a natural aptitude or good, old-fashioned hard work—feels incredible, but make sure you take your success in stride. It's easy to get overconfident or smug about your academic achievements, which paradoxically can make you try less and do worse. If you think you don't need to study for a test and then wind up flunking it, you may come off as lazy and arrogant. Take stock in your success, but remember that there's no "coasting" in life. Things in life don't come easily, and you'll do yourself a disservice by not pushing yourself, even when you're doing well.

YOUR TURN

One way to stay grounded as you succeed (in both school and beyond) is to practice gratitude. Fill in each space with something you're thankful for in life, such as the people (including you!) and things that help you be successful.

GRATITUDE

WHAT'S MADE ME SUCCESSFUL

1 _____

2 _____

3 _____

4 _____

5 _____

6 _____

7 _____

8 _____

9 _____

10 _____

Let Music Center You

There's something really magical about playing an instrument, whether it's the flute, cello, drums, or tambourine. It's not just about making noise (though your parents may argue that's all playing the drums really is); it's also about being creative. Since a lot of instruments (like the trumpet or oboe) require certain breathing techniques, practicing your music is also a natural way to practice being present. In fact, your band instructor has probably already told you about the importance of breathing at the right time, in tempo, on beat. Take that practice one step further and look at how you're sitting (or standing) when you play, how your fingers play the right notes, or how you shape your lips around the mouthpiece to reach that really great high note. And of course, if you play in a band or orchestra, don't just listen to yourself when you play. Make sure you hear how your part fits into the whole, thinking of your instrument as one piece of a much larger tapestry.

YOUR TURN

Record yourself playing as usual, then record yourself playing the same song again but while practicing mindfulness. Did you notice any differences? Did the end result sound different? How did you feel? Jot down your notes.

TAKE 1: REGULAR

NOTES:
_____
_____
_____
_____
_____
_____

TAKE 2: MINDFUL

NOTES:
_____
_____
_____
_____
_____
_____

Be Mindful in Sports

Playing a sport requires coordination, discipline, and a dash of fearlessness. Believe it or not, you can do all that and still be mindful. And don't think being mindful means you have to let the other team win. It's more about tapping into the current moment and being aware of what your body can and can't do. If you're a runner, maybe that means being aware of when you can push yourself one inch farther. Or it could mean staying in the present moment of a football game and not thinking back to the previous play where you fumbled the ball.

A major study found that athletes who utilize mindfulness are often better performers and show better control in and out of the sports arena, so tap into your inner calm and prepare for some great things.

YOUR TURN

Before your next sporting event (game, race, etc.), take time to visualize yourself performing and playing exceptionally. What does this look like to you? Sketch your visualization.

Check in after the event. Did you notice any differences in your performance? Were you more mindful, or did you play better than usual?

My GAME FACE

Embrace the Unknown

From the moment you learned how to talk, people have probably been asking what you want to be when you grow up. Some people simply know from day one that they want to be a doctor, actor, or pastry chef, but for most of us, figuring out how we want to spend the rest of our lives is something of a puzzle. The truth is that you have time to figure out your interests and ambitions, even if it feels like you need to decide before you start applying to colleges. Middle school and high school require a lot of basic classes, so use your curiosity and passion to dig deeper into the ones you're interested in. Or maybe your school offers extracurricular clubs that let you explore interests outside of class. These options could open doors for you down the line that you wouldn't have had access to otherwise. The point is, pursuing your passions and exploring your options are great ways to find out what you want to do when you "grow up."

YOUR TURN

If you're not sure what you want to do in the future, or if you keep changing your mind, that's okay! Becoming aware of what you enjoy and are passionate about are big parts of embracing the unknown and discovering what you want to do. Fill in this Venn diagram to help you identify your passions and talents. In the middle, identify commonalities from both sides. What passions and talents could work together? Are there any careers that use some combination of these passions and talents? Keep an eye out for opportunities that pique your interest, but don't put pressure on yourself to have it all figured out ASAP!

PASSIONS

TALENTS

*In uncertainty, there is comfort. My options—and my mind—
are open to possibilities.*

Take Your Life One Step at a Time

Some of the best advice I ever got regarding my future was from a very wise college counselor: Think only of what you want to do next and figure out how to do it. Don't try to plan out your entire life here and now. That'll drive you crazy! Maybe you want to try something out after college—like travel journalism or politics—but you don't know if it's the perfect fit for you, forever and ever. Is that a problem? Absolutely not! In this day and age, the majority of people don't stay at the same company—let alone in the same field—for more than a few years. It's best to spend your time exploring the next immediate step (scoring well on a test), followed by the next (applying to a great college), followed by the next (running for mayor)—then worry about becoming president of the United States.

YOUR TURN

At the base of the staircase, mark today's date and draw a stick figure of yourself. What's the most current deadline or milestone you need to be focusing on? Don't worry about anything beyond this upcoming deadline. Write this at the top of the stairs, then write down each small step you need to take on each stair leading to your final goal. Each time you complete a step, check the task off on your staircase and draw yourself on that current step!

Taking one small step at a time, I can climb mountains.

CHAPTER 4

STAY CENTERED AND HAPPY:
Self-Esteem and Self-Care

*Personal development isn't about fixing yourself.
You don't need fixing. It's about loving yourself
as you are and evolving because you can.*

—Sam Laura Brown, personal development coach

How do you feel about yourself? How often do you take time to prioritize your own health and wellness? Are you someone who constantly pushes yourself to do your best, running at full speed until you completely run out of gas and burn out, or are you someone who tries their best to find balance in both your daily responsibilities and your overall self-care? You most likely relate to the first example, which is extremely common for teenagers (and adults!). You have so much on your plate every day that it's extremely easy to forget to make time to unwind.

Trying to manage your life without enough self-care can take a toll on you both physically and mentally. You're experiencing so much pressure, and it doesn't help that you're living in the ultimate age of comparison thanks to high expectations from social media. Your self-esteem can take a hit when you don't live up to others' expectations, or the high expectations you set for yourself! The key: Only you can control how you feel, and mindfulness is a big piece of the puzzle that helps you feel good and believe in yourself.

Self-care and self-esteem work together, one helping build the foundation for the other. Throughout this chapter, you'll explore the pillars of self-care and self-confidence, such as how to:

- Practice self-care
- Feel comfortable in your beautiful body
- Embrace who you are
- Take care of your overall health and wellness
- Bring mindfulness to your daily routines
- Practice daily gratitude

It's time to finally build the confidence and self-care foundation you need in order to take high school and the rest of your future by storm. The exercises in this chapter are the perfect way to start!

Practice Self-Care

If you've ever stayed up all night finishing a last-minute assignment or lost shut-eye at a sleepover, you know you won't be running at 100 percent the next day. Maybe you're sleepy, groggy, or even sore and achy. But when you get a good night's sleep, you're (usually) ready to take on the day. Taking care of your mental health is based on the same principles. If you ignore your emotional needs and don't process your feelings and work out your issues, they'll make you feel downright lousy. Luckily, the power of mindfulness meditation can help you take the best care of yourself.

YOUR TURN

Try starting with a five-minute breathing exercise every morning before you get ready for the day. Breathe in for three counts and out for four. Slowly. Relax. Think about all you hope to accomplish during your day and how you'll go about it. And smile!

Every day you try this mindful breathing practice, write down how you feel and the difference it makes on your energy levels. Did you feel refreshed? Rejuvenated? Refocused? Slowly build this activity into your daily habits. You'd be surprised how much even five minutes can change how you feel!

HOW SELF-CARE MAKES ME FEEL

_____

_____

_____

_____

_____

_____

_____

_____

_____

_____

_____

_____

_____

_____

◆ ◆ AFFIRMATION ◆ ◆

This time in the early morning is my own—a wonderful way to focus my body and mind to help me carry out my goals for today.

Keep a Journal

Your moods and emotions are complex, made all the more confusing by the tsunami of hormones crashing into your body right now. Since your moods and emotions are bouncing around in your head all day, they can become mixed up and hard to process. That's why keeping a journal—even if it's just one where you write out the emotions you feel on a particular day—is so important. (If you want to write more, go ahead!) Getting your thoughts down on paper is a fantastic way for you to process and work through the things that are bothering you. An added bonus: It's so cathartic to spend time away from a screen, and, years from now, you'll have a printed reminder that whatever problems you faced weren't, in fact, the end of the world.

YOUR TURN

Never had a journal before? Not sure if it can help? Let's try it out now! In the space here (or in your own journal), write down everything that's on your mind. Try one of these prompts to get your creative juices flowing. Write for at least five minutes, but go longer if you're in the groove! No judgments. Just write.

Now put your pen down and take a deep breath. How did this make you feel? Do you feel lighter or clearer now that you've been able to express something that's been buzzing around your head? If you're intrigued, try to start journaling this week. You can use any old notebook, purchase a special one, or even use your phone or laptop if that's easiest.

JOURNALING PROMPTS

Write down the best moments you experienced today.

_____

_____

_____

Did something bother you today?
What was it, and how did it make you feel?

_____

_____

_____

Who are the people in your life that made today better?

_____

_____

_____

Describe the emotions you felt throughout the day.

_____

_____

_____

✦ ✦ ✦ AFFIRMATION ✦ ✦ ✦

Writing is a way to keep my thoughts organized and to track my progress.

Figure Out What's Going On with Your Body

If you've suffered through the awkwardness that is health class and been forced to watch old afterschool specials, you know that your brain and body are in the middle of a vast metamorphosis. Yeah, it's kind of weird, but it's also unavoidable. You'll get through it, just like billions have before you. It's nothing to be ashamed about!

Mindfulness can help you through this inevitable journey. Start by being aware of how you feel every morning when you wake up. Are you suddenly all arms and legs, tripping over yourself? Does your brain feel fuzzy? Did your voice suddenly drop half an octave? Or maybe you're just feeling especially irritable or cranky thanks to the hormones coursing through your body. Tapping into the root of how you're feeling can help you (figuratively) balance yourself so you can (literally) take on the day ahead.

YOUR TURN

This week, keep track of how you feel both physically and mentally each day. Fill out the weeklong calendar with emojis or similar symbols to represent how you felt each day. This can include good feelings, uncomfortable ones, weird ones, anything!

DAY	FEELING(S)	SAMPLE EMOJIS
S		
M		
T		
W		
T		
F		
S		

Celebrate How Amazing Your Body Is

Sponsored posts, commercials, and social media influencers everywhere tell you that you need to look and act a certain way. Commercials show skinny models laughing on a beach or in a mountain lodge, dressed in perfectly coordinated clothes with glowing complexions and flawless makeup, or men with washboard abs who look like they just stepped out of an action movie. With all these mainstream messages reinforcing the idea that you have to look a certain way, it can be hard to accept your body for what it is. Instead of constantly comparing yourself to celebrities or social media posts, celebrate what your body can do for you—whether that's climb mountains, fight off colds, do cartwheels, solve a difficult calculus problem, or feel rested and refreshed after a good night's sleep. Remember, your body is your own and isn't dictated by what someone else thinks it should be!

YOUR TURN

For various parts of your body (arms, hands, legs, heart, etc.), use and finish this prompt: "I am eternally grateful for my _____ (SAY YOUR BODY PART HERE) because it helps me _____ (SAY WHAT THAT BODY PART HELPS YOU ACCOMPLISH)." For example, "I am eternally grateful for my hands because they helped me type this book!" The next time you're feeling self-conscious or having negative thoughts about your body, return to this page and remind yourself of at least one thing you're grateful for. Your body is doing so much every day to simply keep you alive and well. Honor and treasure it.

I am eternally grateful for my _____
because it helps me _____
_____
_____ .

I am eternally grateful for my _____
because it helps me _____
_____
_____ .

I am eternally grateful for my _____
because it helps me _____
_____
_____ .

I am eternally grateful for my _____
because it helps me _____
_____
_____ .

◆ ◆ ◆ **AFFIRMATION** ◆ ◆ ◆

My body is my own. From my head to my toes I am me,
and I am greater than the sum of my parts.

Turn Negatives Into Positives

Feeling good about yourself has to come from inside of you. But what if you're constantly thinking about yourself in a negative light? That negative self-talk is holding you back from being truly confident and feeling wonderful about yourself. When you look in the mirror, don't analyze what you dislike or focus on a part of yourself you might change if you could. Think beyond the idea that the only "acceptably beautiful" people are women who are blonde, tall, and thin, or men who are tall, toned, tanned, and strong. Accept your body—and everyone else's—for what it is! Negative self-speak is a slippery slope, and one that can cause a lot of pain. Instead, break yourself out of that cycle. Start thinking of all your great traits—not just the physical ones but all the things that make you uniquely you. As you repeat those to yourself time and time again, those thoughts become a talisman against the pressures of the outside world.

YOUR TURN

It's time to turn those negative thoughts into positive ones. In the left column, write down any negative thoughts you notice yourself thinking. In the right column, flip the script and write something positive about the thing you're being critical of. For example, if you're constantly thinking "I have a big nose, therefore it's ugly," you can turn this into a positive by saying "My nose is a unique and powerful asset that makes me the beautiful person I am."

NEGATIVE *Thoughts* ➡ POSITIVE *Thoughts*

_____ _____
_____ _____
_____ _____
_____ _____
_____ _____
_____ _____
_____ _____
_____ _____
_____ _____
_____ _____
_____ _____
_____ _____
_____ _____
_____ _____
_____ _____
_____ _____
_____ _____

◆◆ AFFIRMATION ◆◆

*I feel good about myself and deserve to treat
myself with respect and care.*

Listen to Your Body

Our bodies know what they need, but sometimes we forget to listen. One of the most common cravings our bodies have that many of us ignore is the need for enough sleep. We push ourselves as much as possible every day, wanting to stay up late to either watch TV, reply to friends on Snapchat, or cram for an important test. When you start practicing mindfulness in your everyday life, you'll start noticing the signs your body tries to send you when it requires its basic needs, such as sleep, food, and water. Instead of skipping meals, staying up late, or drinking more soda, start paying attention to how you feel throughout the day and actually give your body what it needs.

YOUR TURN

Use the following scenarios to create a plan for how you'll respond when your body starts to feel certain ways. For example, if you start to feel fatigued at night, you can plan to put down your phone and turn off the lights to try to sleep. Keep what you write down in mind as you go about your daily routine, and remember to be mindful of actually listening to your body when it needs your attention in order to stay healthy and strong.

When I feel fatigued, I will _____

_____

_____

When I feel overwhelmed, I will _____

_____

_____

When I feel bloated, I will _____

_____

_____

When my mouth feels dry, I will _____

_____

_____

When my stomach starts aching and grumbling, I will

_____

_____

Feel Good at Any Size

If you've ever gone shopping and felt supremely frustrated about the limited size options—jeans that don't come in tall or short, tops that mysteriously aren't made beyond a certain size, shoes that aren't wide enough—you're not alone. It can be especially hard if there's a certain style you really want but that doesn't come in your size. Your first reaction might be anger or shock—why can't they just make more diverse sizes? Or it might be shame that you can't fit into the limited options available. Neither of these thoughts is constructive. Instead, visit a different store or find a clothing line that fits your body and offers pieces that show off your personality. Stressing about your size does more harm than good. Look at each day as a fresh start and, if getting healthier or losing weight is one of your goals, think positively about how you'll reach it in a productive, healthful way.

The same goes for how you treat others. Just as you shouldn't judge yourself, don't judge others by their looks—you'll miss out on their other lovely traits. Judging people by their character is a much better way to live your life, and people will respect and admire you for it.

YOUR TURN

Picture in your head your absolute dream outfit. What's something that would help you feel AMAZING? Grab some colored pencils, crayons, or markers and design this dream outfit of yours. Bring the mental picture you have to life on the page!

MY DREAM OUTFIT

◆ · ◆ · AFFIRMATION · ◆ · ◆

I am more than the size of my clothes or the number on my scale.

Eat Mindfully

Think of this scenario: You're at the movies with a group of friends and you've decided to partake in one of the great joys of movie theaters—the concession stand. Maybe you and a friend decide to split some snacks, like a 64-ounce tub of popcorn, a giant bag of gummy bears, and a bottomless soda. Halfway through the movie your friend reaches over for some of the popcorn you've been hoarding only to find you've somehow eaten almost the entire tub without even thinking about it.

When you don't think about what you're putting into your body, it's easy to shovel whatever's in front of you into your mouth. That's an awful way to eat, mostly because you end up feeling sick to your stomach after devouring something like a metric ton of buttered popcorn. Mindful eating—much like mindfulness itself—is about being present. You can practice mindful eating any number of ways, like taking smaller bites and spending more time chewing while focusing on the texture and taste of the food. Also ask yourself if you're truly hungry or simply bored to keep from snacking mindlessly. These are small changes that can help you be not only healthier but happier.

YOUR TURN

Draw a picture of your favorite meal or food. This can be a snack, dinner, drink, your favorite thing to order at a restaurant, anything! One requirement: Be mindful as you do it. Really notice how you're feeling when you draw, the texture of the paper, the sounds around you, etc.

When you finish, ask yourself how it felt. The next time you have a meal or snack, use the same type of mindset and see if it makes you feel any different. Start building the habit of eating or drinking mindfully, noticing how much more aware you are of what you're consuming, enjoying the experience and the taste of your food, and observing if you feel sick to your stomach as often compared to when you mindlessly eat everything in a rush.

◆ ◆ ◆ AFFIRMATION ◆ ◆ ◆

What I put into my body is directly related to what I can get out of it. I will make an effort to savor every spoonful and be thankful for the food in front of me.

Stay Hydrated

Not all mindfulness has to be about some deep, spiritual awakening. It's also about the basics, like drinking water! Being mindful helps you be attuned to what your body's telling you. Thirst can show up in lots of different ways. Are you feeling lethargic? Do you have a headache? Are you experiencing digestive issues? You might just be thirsty. Be sure to drink plenty of water every day (doctors say around eight glasses). It's a simple task but one that will keep you looking—and feeling—better for years to come.

YOUR TURN

This week, keep track of how many glasses of water you drink each day and take notes about how you feel.

TIP: Fill in the glasses with water

DAY	AMOUNT OF WATER I DRANK	HOW I FELT
S		
M		

DAY	AMOUNT OF WATER I DRANK	HOW I FELT
T		
W		
T		
F		
S		

Take a Mindful Walk

There's nothing like going for a long, relaxing walk, especially when the weather is great and there's a gentle breeze. Being mindful while you walk is easy—just put away your phone and earbuds and instead focus on how each step feels as you transfer your weight from the ball of your foot to your other heel, right foot, left foot, repeat. Feel how your joints respond and how your muscles gradually loosen up the longer you walk. Take in your surroundings, looking up at skyscrapers or trees depending on where you are. Let your mind wander where it will and get into a rhythm. No one says you have to be still to be mindful. And remember that a walking meditation isn't just good for your mind—it's good for your whole body!

YOUR TURN

The next time you go for a walk, be mindful and take note of what each of your five senses experiences. How are you feeling? What can you hear? Did you notice anything different during this mindful walk compared to your usual strolls? Draw yourself taking your most recent walk and create an image of your favorite moments experienced through each of your five senses. Were there birds chirping in the trees? Some sweet-smelling flowers you never noticed before? Each time you go on a walk, try to discover something new!

WHAT I SEE

WHAT I SMELL

WHAT I HEAR

WHAT I FEEL

WHAT I TASTE

◆ ◆ ◆ **AFFIRMATION** ◆ ◆ ◆

One foot, then the other. Peace, then understanding.

Stretch Out

There's nothing more satisfying than a nice, long, luxurious stretch after being hunched over a desk for most of the day, but it's hard to prioritize time to stretch with everything else you've got going on. Try this: Any time you've been sitting for more than an hour, stand up and stretch. Put your hands over your head, arch your back, and twist your torso from side to side. Basically, do whatever feels good! Doing so not only keeps you loose and limber; it also feels great and helps increase blood flow to your muscles. What's not to love about that?

If you're settling in for a long study session, set a timer on your phone, watch, or computer to get up at least once an hour to stretch and move. After trying this, did you notice any difference? Were you able to concentrate for longer than usual? Did your body feel better?

YOUR TURN

Use the image on the following page to remind yourself of some simple stretches you can do to loosen up when you've been sitting for a while. Add your own favorites to the drawing.

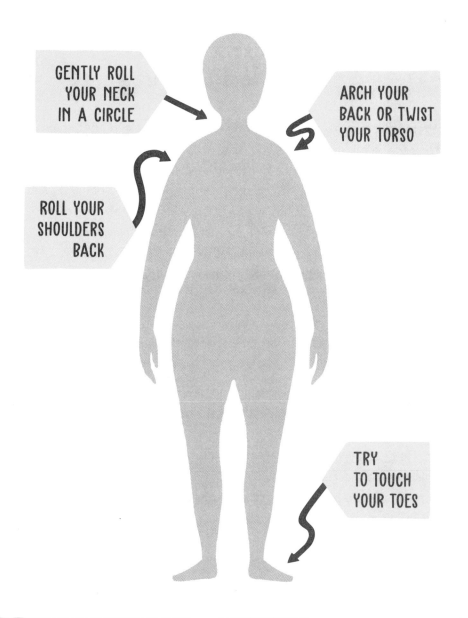

GENTLY ROLL
YOUR NECK
IN A CIRCLE

ARCH YOUR
BACK OR TWIST
YOUR TORSO

ROLL YOUR
SHOULDERS
BACK

TRY
TO TOUCH
YOUR TOES

◆◆ AFFIRMATION ◆◆

Keeping my body elastic helps my mind to stay limber as well.

Try a Five-Minute Mini-Meditation

There will be some days when you feel like you just can't get up early to practice mindfulness or you're so busy that it's hard to find time during the day to be present. It's not ideal, but it is understandable!

When you feel pressed for time, simply do a quick check-in and remember your breathing. Are you breathing deeply or are your breaths shallow? Are you holding tension in your face, neck, shoulders, or belly? If so, take five minutes to do the following easy three-step meditation. It's like a small reset button that will help you stay focused and centered.

YOUR TURN

Still don't think you've got five minutes? If you check your social media feeds one less time during the day, you'll recapture five minutes, no problem. Then follow the steps for the five-minute meditation on the following page.

That's it! How do you feel? Refocused? A little refreshed? Keep this in mind the next time you're feeling overwhelmed by your busy schedule. You'd be surprised how much of a difference something so small can make!

FIVE-MINUTE
MINI-MEDITATION

1 Write down three things you're thankful for in this moment:

1 _____

2 _____

3 _____

2 Take five deep breaths in and out, keeping all the things from your list close to your heart.

3 Rotate your shoulders back as you start thinking about the present moment.

◆ ◆ **AFFIRMATION** ◆ ◆

Using my breath to keep me centered, I can quickly refocus my energy.

Use Your Time Wisely

The last time you were stuck in a long line, what did you do? Tap your foot impatiently? Bury your head in your phone? Sigh loudly about the grand injustice of it all? While those may all be ways to pass the time, they're not exactly productive. Sure, it's tempting to get some extra time in on Snapchat, but next time, challenge yourself to be present. Take in everything around you. It won't help the line move any more quickly, but changing your perspective about an inevitable nuisance is just as important as making it to the front of the line.

YOUR TURN

The next time you're waiting in line, whether to get food, buy something at the store, or something else, be mindful of the people around you. Without staring awkwardly, see if there's anyone in particular you find interesting or mysterious. If so, use your imagination to come up with a backstory for that person. What do you think this person's life might be like? What led them to be in line with you today? Write a story about them and their journey to the exact moment of your mindfulness practice.

Whenever you're stuck waiting in line, instead of trying to distract yourself to pass the time, be mindful, take deep breaths, and don't forget to use your imagination!

Find Mindfulness in Your Morning Routine

Getting ready every day can be boring. Brushing your teeth, combing your hair, and that whole annoying business of showering—it's impossible to multitask while doing that stuff, right? Nope! Aside from wanting to look (and smell) your best, you can also use the time you spend getting ready being mindful. If you usually zone out while brushing your teeth, try instead to think of all the ways you're helping yourself by having a sparkling smile—for example, needing fewer trips to the dentist. Your goal is simply focusing on the task at hand. Instead of whipping your comb through your hair, focus on the act of combing, not thinking of the other ten things you have to do this morning.

YOUR TURN

What is your typical morning routine for getting ready for school? Write down each task, how long it takes you to complete them (when you aren't running late and trying to rush out the door!), and ways you can be mindful while doing them (ways to use your senses and be in the present moment). For example, when brushing your teeth, you can notice the taste and smell of the toothpaste, the sound of the brushing, and the feel of the bristles on your gums. After thinking of all the ways you can be mindful during these tasks, try them out and take note of how you feel.

MY MORNING ROUTINE

ACTIVITY	TIME	WAYS TO BE MINDFUL		

◆ ◆ AFFIRMATION ◆ ◆

Even when brushing my teeth or combing my hair,
I pay attention to the task at hand.

Feel Better on Bad Days

Even if you're a positive person, some days inside your brain are just going to be dreary. When that happens, remind yourself that this feeling is only temporary. When that day is done and over with, you'll get to start a whole new day that carries the promise of being better than the last. If you're bummed about something or just can't shake the blues, try thinking of a happy memory or an upcoming adventure. It could be looking forward to a spring break trip or recalling a really great memory with your family. Whatever the cause, realize it's okay to feel blue, and that, in time, the sun will emerge from behind the clouds and everything will be better than it is right now.

YOUR TURN

If you're feeling blue, try thinking of one positive thing right now. It could be something small, like the fact that you woke up this morning, or maybe you're just having a good hair day. Write down your one positive thing and take a moment to meditate on this glimmer of light.

Take some deep breaths, then try to add more things to your list. Keep doing this until you've completely run out of happy things to write about. (If you can only think of the one thing, that's okay! Don't judge yourself.) Now look at your small reminders that there's still some sunshine even when you're feeling blue. You will be okay.

GOOD THINGS

THAT HAPPENED TODAY

_____

_____

_____

_____

_____

_____

_____

_____

_____

_____

_____

_____

◆ ◆ AFFIRMATION ◆ ◆

There's nothing wrong with feeling blue.
I know that clouds sometimes cover the sun, and there's beauty in that.
There's also comfort in knowing the clouds won't be there forever.

Find Gratitude Every Day

You've probably already heard about the importance of gratitude and focusing on the positive things in your life, but what does that actually mean? Isn't it enough that you're grateful once a year during Thanksgiving dinner? Well, not really. Even on a boring, average day, remember to reflect. Are you thankful for that text your friend sent you that made you feel special? Did someone at lunch let you take the last slice of pizza? Small, seemingly inconsequential things are the threads of thankfulness, and you can weave those threads into a strong daily practice.

YOUR TURN

Fill in these hearts with things you're thankful for. The more you practice, the easier it'll become! You can continue your daily practice in your journal or sketchbook after you fill in these hearts.

I'M GRATEFUL FOR...

Celebrate Your Successes

There are some days when everything's going great. You aced a test, had a fabulous date, or received some good news. That's fantastic! You should celebrate! Reflecting on all of your recent successes (big or small!) is an important mindfulness activity to remind yourself that you're progressing toward your goals. This perspective can help when you feel like you're not moving forward on any big projects or dreams. Even if you're taking small steps, you're further along today than you were yesterday!

YOUR TURN

What are some successes you've had lately? Have you taken time to celebrate them yet? If not, it's time to create a celebration list! Write down a couple of key successes or good things happening in your life, along with a way to celebrate them. It can be something as small as throwing a solo dance party in your room with some of your favorite music! Refer back to this list to reward yourself and to help you appreciate the positive parts of your life even more.

LET'S CELEBRATE!

WHY I'M CELEBRATING:

_____

_____

WHAT THE CELEBRATION WILL BE:

_____

_____

WHEN IT WILL BE:

_____

HOW I WILL PLAN AND EXECUTE IT:

_____

_____

_____

WHO WILL COME:

_____

_____

_____

LET'S CELEBRATE!

WHY I'M CELEBRATING:

_____

_____

WHAT THE CELEBRATION WILL BE:

_____

_____

WHEN IT WILL BE:

_____

HOW I WILL PLAN AND EXECUTE IT:

_____

_____

_____

WHO WILL COME:

_____

_____

◆ ◆ AFFIRMATION ◆ ◆

Every day is a new chance to feel thankful, happy, and fulfilled by all the positive things in my life.

Deal with Anxiety

From tests to friendship drama to a fear of failure, you probably have a million things that make you anxious. Plus, your future might feel uncertain as you and your friends change and life goes from familiar to unknown. Maybe you don't know where you want to go to college or what you want to do with the rest of your time in middle school and high school—and beyond.

Some smaller anxiety problems can be sorted out relatively easily with simple changes like making your diet healthier or adding exercise to your routine (we'll talk about that in the next entry), but other problems require more thought and care (and possibly professional help from a doctor or therapist). It's okay to not have all the answers or to be unsure about your future. It's also okay to worry every once in a while. Sometimes reflecting can help you feel more determined to find a solution. Whatever your worry, anxiety can be greatly lessened by being mindful.

YOUR TURN

Create a word cloud of the anxious emotions you're currently experiencing, making the stronger emotions larger and the less prominent feelings smaller. What are the two or three largest emotions you wrote in your word cloud? (See the Cope with a Growing Family exercise for an example of a word cloud.) What do you think may be causing these feelings? Who can you reach out to for help in navigating these emotions? Sometimes discussing how you're feeling with loved ones can help clear your mind and make you feel more at ease about what you're going through. Take deep breaths and remind yourself that you're going to be okay.

MY ANXIOUS FEELINGS WORD CLOUD

◆ ◆ ◆ AFFIRMATION ◆ ◆ ◆

I will not let my anxiety get the best of me. There are parts of my life that may be uncertain or unclear, but I will embrace those as challenges and opportunities to grow stronger.

Cope with Anxiety's Physical Symptoms

Let's talk about how anxiety affects your body. You could feel a sick feeling in your stomach when you forget to study for a test, cold sweats when you realize you left your term paper at home, or problems sleeping because you're replaying an unpleasant interaction with a friend in your mind. Here are some things that may help:

- Try breathing exercises to help you recenter and calm yourself.
- Go for a walk around your neighborhood.
- Cook a meal for your family.
- Pamper yourself with a warm bath to help your muscles relax.

While you're doing these exercises, remind yourself that anxiety is just another problem to be solved.

YOUR TURN

When you're feeling anxious or stressed, how do you usually feel it physically? Do you get butterflies in your stomach, headaches, the shakes, or does your breathing speed up? Use this stick figure to label what you feel and where you feel it most. The more you practice mindfulness, the more aware you'll be when you feel those mental stresses causing physical pain.

How do you usually try to calm down and take care of your body when you notice yourself feeling this way? Under each label on the stick figure, write down at least one way you can help soothe what you experience when you feel anxious or stressed. This can include breathing mindfully, stretching, or drinking more water.

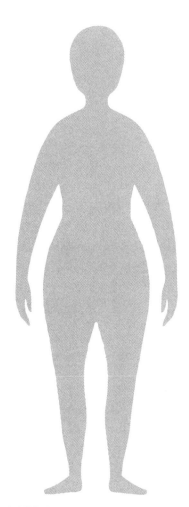

ADDRESSING ANXIETY SYMPTOMS

◆ ◆ AFFIRMATION ◆ ◆

*Anxiety affects not only my mind but also my body.
Being mindful, I will take care of my whole person in a way
that helps reduce stress and improve my well-being.*

Learn to Let Go of Anger

Anger is a wide-ranging emotion, spanning from being mildly annoyed at something to frustration to a full-blown blinding rage that makes it hard to think. But let's be clear: Being angry isn't "wrong," but it also isn't something to brush under the rug. Plus, sometimes you can channel your anger in a healthy way, like standing up for what's right in the face of adversity. If you're always in a rage, stomping around and feeling like the world has wronged you, it's probably time to step back and take a deeper look at the source of your anger. Once you've identified it, try to let go of the situation that made you livid in the first place and look ahead to the future. This doesn't mean you're condoning someone's bad behavior, but it does mean you won't let it bother you any longer.

YOUR TURN

Imagine that the anger you feel is weighing you down like an anchor chained to your body. Write what's making you furious in the anchor. To free yourself from this anchor, write down at least three thoughts in the space outside the anchor that can help you move forward, such as "I didn't like how this felt, but I want to move on."

I harbor a quiet peace inside.
In learning to let go of my anger, I'm no longer weighed down by the past.

Address Moments of Jealousy

At its roots, jealousy is petty and only breeds ill will and bitterness. This can be a difficult emotion to own up to, but observing it will help you overcome it. If you're feeling jealous, notice the feelings and try not to judge yourself. When you've calmed down, ask yourself what you're really jealous of. The attention someone's getting? A material thing another person has that you don't? Chances are you have plenty of good things going on in your own life that you may not even realize—don't be afraid to take a moment to reflect on all you do have! Being mindful of your circumstances (and blessings!) is a powerful way to protect yourself against this ugly green-eyed monster.

YOUR TURN

One of the best ways to notice thoughts fueled by jealousy and stopping them in their tracks is by practicing mindfulness and turning toward gratitude. If a few people come to mind whom you may feel a little jealous of, try to start changing those thoughts into something like cheering the other person on for their accomplishments and feeling gratitude for what you have in your own life right now. Use the prompts on the next page to guide you through this process.

Example: "Instead of feeling jealous about Sophie going on vacation to Italy, I'll think that I'm super excited for her because I know how much she loves to travel. Plus, I'm thankful for the opportunities to explore new and exciting places nearby until I'm able to go farther abroad."

Instead of feeling jealous about _____

_____

(PERSON'S NAME AND WHAT YOU'RE JEALOUS ABOUT),
I'll think _____

_____

(POSITIVE THOUGHT ABOUT THE PERSON). Plus, I'm thankful for

_____

_____(SOMETHING POSITIVE IN YOUR LIFE).

Instead of feeling jealous about _____

_____

(PERSON'S NAME AND WHAT YOU'RE JEALOUS ABOUT),
I'll think _____

_____

(POSITIVE THOUGHT ABOUT THE PERSON). Plus, I'm thankful for

_____

_____(SOMETHING POSITIVE IN YOUR LIFE).

◆◆ AFFIRMATION ◆◆

The opposites of jealousy are contentment and calm. When I feel jealous about something or someone, I'll let calmness and contentment wash over me, constantly being happy for others and thankful for what I have.

Build Self-Confidence

Have you ever heard the phrase "fake it till you make it"? Think of how many people have used this idea over the course of history. Do you think every president, CEO, and multiplatinum singer has always had extreme confidence in themselves? No way! They have moments of doubt too, but they learn how to overcome them. Lucky for you, self-confidence is something that can be learned (and, yes, faked until you believe it). Here are two major tips:

1 **Stop the negative self-talk.** If you failed at something, don't call yourself worthless or a failure. It's okay not to succeed. You tried your best, and you'll do better next time.

2 **Stand tall, pull your shoulders back, and smile.** Most people wouldn't believe someone shuffling around with sad, sloped shoulders is saturated in self-confidence, but they *would* believe someone with a genuine smile and good posture knows what's what. Sometimes, if you believe that you believe it, soon enough it'll be true.

YOUR TURN

What's an area of your life you feel confident about? It could be your skill at a sport, your ability in a certain subject in school, or a skill you have, like drawing. Write what you're confident about at the top of the tower, then label some bricks with the reasons you feel good about it. Maybe it's the hours you've spent practicing, maybe it's the good grades that reflect a job well done, or maybe it's receiving compliments from others. When you run into an area of your life where you don't feel as confident, ask yourself what bricks would help you build toward accomplishing that goal?

◇ ◇ AFFIRMATION ◇ ◇

Head up, shoulders back, smile on:
My secret weapons for achieving self-confidence.

Deal with Bullies

Every school has them: the group of kids who pick on the shrimpy nerd, the gaggle of mean girls who judge your clothes or hair, or that person who always makes snarky comments on your Instagram posts. Bullies are, sadly, something you'll probably have to deal with many times throughout your life. While all fifty states have laws against it, bullying remains a constant problem.

Mindfulness can really help both parties in this situation. First, take time to process and mitigate your emotions, no matter which side you're on. (Everyone makes mistakes, and even the best of us might temporarily play the role of bully, as much as we hate to admit it.) How, as the victim, does bullying make you feel? When you take away your bully's power to make you feel less than you are, you're the true victor. On the other hand, how, as the bully, do you feel when you say something mean or derogatory? Are you even aware you're making others angry or sad? Using the techniques in this book can help you react more positively to challenging situations.

And, of course, it's extremely important to tell a parent or teacher if you're being bullied.

YOUR TURN

If you're being bullied or notice yourself bullying someone else, take some time to think about how you're feeling. Are you angry? Is this really about the other person? What kind of events lead to these moments? Think about all the mindfulness tips and practices you've learned in this book. What are some ways you can use mindfulness to help you stay centered during this experience?

MY THOUGHTS

Embrace Your Shyness

If someone's ever called on you in a public situation (in class, at a birthday party, or at an event) and you found yourself shrinking into your seat, hoping to vanish, congratulations! You're shy! First off, don't think of shyness as a problem to be fixed—it isn't a fatal flaw or something for which you should judge yourself. It's simply a part of who you are. Instead of beating yourself up about it, accept that shyness is part of your personality and that it's fine! You can also use your self-awareness to reflect on exactly what makes you nervous about certain social situations. Try acting out upcoming situations in your head ahead of time—it might help you gather the confidence you need to approach them without feeling as anxious. Take a deep breath, relax, and smile. You're ready.

YOUR TURN

Did you know your shyness can be your strength? While it's easy to focus on viewing shyness as a weakness, let's focus on how it can be your secret weapon. What are some ways your beautiful introversion can be an advantage? What opportunities have arrived because you were a little shy? Fill in these prompts to remind yourself of all the good things your personality brings you.

If there are any specific scenarios where you'd like to be more confident in the future, take time to meditate on ways you can approach these situations differently the next time around.

SHYNESS *is a* STRENGTH

I may be shy, but it helps me

_____

_____

_____

_____ .

I may be shy, but it helps me

_____

_____

_____

_____ .

I may be shy, but it helps me

_____

_____

_____

_____ .

I may be shy, but it helps me

_____

_____

_____

_____ .

I may be shy, but it helps me

_____

_____

_____

_____ .

◆ ◆ AFFIRMATION ◆ ◆

I accept myself for who I am, without judgment.

CHAPTER 5

WELCOME WHAT'S AHEAD:
Your Bright Future

*Authenticity is the daily practice of
letting go of who we think we're supposed
to be and embracing who we are.*

—Brené Brown, PhD, LMSW, professor, and bestselling author

As you navigate life, you probably find yourself often being encouraged to be more like other people. Whether you want to look more like one of your favorite celebrities, wish you had the life of someone on TikTok, or hope that you someday have as many followers as the most popular girl in school, the reality is you will never find true happiness until you truly own and embrace being your authentic self. Getting caught in the comparison trap is easy, but now is the time to listen to your inner voice and be brave enough to be who you want to be in this world.

That sounds great in theory, but being yourself can be scary! Some people might try to bring you down when you start living the life you truly want. If that happens, know that they come from a place of jealousy and insecurity. You are enough, and you deserve to be yourself. The journey of self-discovery isn't easy, but using mindfulness and self-care along the way will help you grow even more. This is exactly what you'll learn throughout this chapter, while covering topics such as:

- Overcoming and facing your fears
- Discovering your purpose and passions
- Understanding your values and what's important to you
- Unplugging and not overworking yourself
- Handling social media in a healthy way
- Looking forward to the future

This is the final piece of your mindfulness journey in this book. You've worked through how to bring mindfulness and self-care to your relationships, home, school, and self-confidence. It's time to take everything you've learned and apply it to this final chapter to help you take the world by storm and to be happy, be calm, and, ultimately, be YOU!

Step Out of the Approval Matrix

The name of the game in middle school and high school is trying to fit in. So many movies and TV shows deal with kids in school trying to do just that, with each of the characters looking—on some level—for approval. In some situations, they desperately want validation; others seem like they don't really care, but you later learn that, deep down, it's a driving force. Here's the thing, though: The characters always find out at the end that (spoiler alert!) they didn't need approval from their peers because they were special and unique to begin with. Plus, when you stop looking for approval and start living as your authentic, wonderful self, the right friends and relationships will start to appear. Focus your energy on being the best possible person you can be—kind, loving, caring, energetic, weird, quirky, etc.—and you'll start attracting people into your life that love and appreciate you for who you truly are.

YOUR TURN

Have you noticed yourself wanting to be like other people or to be accepted by a specific group of people? If you're not sure, be mindful when you're talking to different classmates at school. Do you ever try to hide certain parts of you or act differently when you talk to certain people? Don't judge yourself. It's natural to want to be liked and accepted by others. Write down any observations you make.

Now think of the parts of you that you tend to hide from certain people. Do you have any family or friends who *do* accept those sides of you? Ask them why they like those things about you. It may remind you that they're also part of what makes you special and wonderful!

PARTS OF MYSELF I SOMETIMES HIDE

_____

_____

_____

_____

_____

_____

_____

PEOPLE WHO ACCEPT ME FOR WHO I AM

_____

_____

_____

_____

_____

_____

_____

_____

·◆·◆· AFFIRMATION ·◆·◆·

Rather than waste my energy seeking validation, I'll use my time to accept my authentic self and, in doing so, will naturally find friends who like me for who I truly am.

Overcome Fear-Based Thinking

Life's unknowns can be paralyzing if you let them sit front of mind all the time (Will we get into a car crash? Will I get kidnapped?). Early humans developed fear as a primal response to keep us alive and safe from danger, like attacks by wild animals. These days, our bodies can have that same chemical response even if the danger isn't real. Fear-based thinking is problematic not only because it doesn't let you enjoy life, but also because it's a vicious, unrelenting cycle that affects how you feel. The more you allow your mind to entertain fear-based thoughts, the more they spiral out of control.

The good news is that your brain can change. How? Practice deep-breathing exercises to calm yourself. Simply asking yourself why you're fearful can help separate perceived threats from actual threats or help you decide how likely a certain outcome really is. Little by little, you can help yourself go from a state of fear to one of calm.

YOUR TURN

First, let's focus on specific situations that you know bring you anxiety. Is it public speaking? Learning to drive? Write down the thoughts you usually have when you experience anxiety in this situation and see if you can identify where these fearful thoughts are coming from. Did something happen before that you're afraid might happen again? Did it happen to someone else? Are you scared of failing?

Now let's take those fear-based thought patterns and literally rewrite them. For each sentence you wrote, write the opposite, more positive approach to the situation. For example: If you're terrified of giving speeches in class and are thinking "I'm going to mess up what

I say and the whole class will laugh at me," rewrite it as "I'm going to speak clearly and effectively and my teacher will be impressed." Studies show that retraining your thoughts in this way does have an effect on how you view and approach the world!

SITUATIONS THAT MAKE ME ANXIOUS AND WHY

1 _____

2 _____

3 _____

POSITIVE WAYS TO LOOK AT THOSE SITUATIONS

1 _____

2 _____

3 _____

◆ ◆ ◆ AFFIRMATION ◆ ◆ ◆

Easing my fears, I become calm.
I allow myself to be present and free of toxic thoughts.

Get to Sleep Faster

Ever had one of those nights (or many of them) where you're tossing and turning, thoughts racing, and you can't get to sleep no matter what? We've all been there. Being present can help you drift off into dreamland because you'll stop your mind from worrying about what's happened in the past or what might happen in the future. Instead, focus on the here and now. If this happens to you frequently, try out some time-tested ways to mindfully ease into sleep, such as following a guided meditation, practicing breathing techniques, and listening to calming music. (Notice what's not on this list: staring at your phone!) Find the method that works best for you.

YOUR TURN

Not sure where to start? Try the following breathing method by Harvard-trained physician Dr. Andrew Weil. When done continually over a few minutes, your body will naturally calm itself and release any tension you might have. Since you're focusing on your breathing and not your cares and concerns, you can drift away worry-free. Then fill in the list with other things that might help you fall asleep.

DR. WEIL'S BREATHING EXERCISE

1 Breathe in for four counts.
2 Hold your breath in for seven counts.
3 Slowly breathe out for eight counts.

IDEAS TO HELP ME FALL ASLEEP

◇ ◆ ◇ AFFIRMATION ◇ ◆ ◇

Using my breath, I ease my way into a deep, restful, and restorative sleep.

Sleep Better

There's a reason why "sleep like a baby" is such a popular phrase. When you're born, you literally don't have a care in the world beyond hunger, and maybe the hope that you'll get mashed pears over mushy peas for dinner. As you grow up, your responsibilities and worries begin to weigh on you, creating anxiety and making it much harder to "sleep like a baby."

There's a solution, though: using mindfulness to trigger what Harvard doctor Herbert Benson, director emeritus of the Benson-Henry Institute for Mind Body Medicine at Massachusetts General Hospital, calls the "relaxation response." The relaxation response is the opposite of the stress response, which causes your body to tense up and generally feel awful. Going to sleep when you're in a state of worry-free bliss will yield a better night's rest than, say, collapsing into an exhausted heap after hours of fretting. Your cares and problems might still be there in the morning, but you can better face the day knowing you've got the power (and power reserves) to take them on.

YOUR TURN

Having a nightly routine can help you trigger a relaxation response and get you back to sleeping like a baby! This routine doesn't have to be a big process—even one simple mindfulness practice a night before going to bed can help reduce stress and improve your quality of sleep. Write down the steps you take now under Current Routine. (Be honest with yourself. It's okay if your current nightly routine only consists of turning off your phone and crawling into bed!)

Looking at your current routine, do you see anything you think you should change? Could you journal, breathe, or meditate to help yourself wind down and destress from the day? Write down your revamped routine under New Routine.

CURRENT ROUTINE	NEW ROUTINE

After a week of your new routine, did you notice any differences? Did you fall asleep more quickly or have a more restful sleep, or did nothing change? Should you revisit your routine and try something new? Your nighttime routine can be an ever-changing experience. Find what helps you the most!

✦✦ AFFIRMATION ✦✦

I am calm and relaxed. Sleep comes easily to me every night.

Wake Up with Purpose

Mornings can be painful. The alarm goes off way too early, you keep hitting snooze, and you end up rushing because you waited too long to get ready. But it doesn't have to be that way! When your alarm goes off, try lying in bed for a few moments, consciously feeling your breath and beginning to feel your body. Notice the position in which you've been sleeping. Start wiggling your toes and slowly stretching your muscles. As you start to feel more awake, focus your energy on the task at hand—getting ready for the day—and how you'll tackle the obstacles before you. There's no guarantee this will make you like mornings any better, but at least you'll be approaching them calmly.

YOUR TURN

Not a morning person? That's okay! Let's start working toward appreciating mornings with some positive thinking. Under the bright and cheery morning sky, write down some of the beautiful things that come with mornings! For example, sunshine, birds chirping, fresh coffee (or tea, or juice!), your favorite breakfast foods...it can be anything!

THINGS TO LOVE ABOUT MORNINGS

◆ ◆ ◆ AFFIRMATION ◆ ◆ ◆

When my alarm goes off, I remind myself to wake up with purpose, being mindful of my body and how I transition from sleeping to waking life.

Find Downtime

These days, everyone seems to have calendars filled to the brim with activities. Interpretive dance practice on Mondays, tae kwon do lessons on Tuesdays, volunteering at the animal shelter on Wednesdays, debate team practice after school on Thursdays, two-hour study sessions on Fridays, and babysitting or working on big group projects on the weekends. While it's great to be busy, sometimes we put too much pressure on ourselves to do it all.

There's something to be said about being able to gracefully say no to an activity or event and giving yourself time to relax and be a teenager! There's so much emphasis on academic and extracurricular performance, much of it with good reason, but remember: You can only be your best self when you give yourself time to recharge. Read a book for fun, go to the movies, go ice skating with friends, or give yourself permission to do nothing at all! Not everything is about a means to an end, and remembering to pace yourself is priceless.

YOUR TURN

Look at your schedule for the upcoming week. If it's a busy one (like most of your weeks!), choose an exact date and time when you'll make downtime a priority. (Even better if you can choose multiple times!) And it doesn't have to be something huge. It can be as simple as taking thirty minutes to read a book or practicing mindfulness with journaling and meditation. Make a promise to yourself to commit to this reserved time with the following permission slips.

Permission Slip

I, _____ (YOUR NAME), promise to
take _____ (PERIOD OF TIME) of my day on
_____ (DATE) at _____ (TIME)
to spend time _____
_____
_____ (YOUR FAVORITE ACTIVITY).

Permission Slip

I, _____ (YOUR NAME), promise to
take _____ (PERIOD OF TIME) of my day on
_____ (DATE) at _____ (TIME)
to spend time _____
_____
_____ (YOUR FAVORITE ACTIVITY).

Permission Slip

I, _____ (YOUR NAME), promise to
take _____ (PERIOD OF TIME) of my day on
_____ (DATE) at _____ (TIME)
to spend time _____
_____
_____ (YOUR FAVORITE ACTIVITY).

♦ ♦ ♦ AFFIRMATION ♦ ♦ ♦

Rest, recharge, rejoice.
Not everything is about getting ahead or competing.

Do More by Doing Less

Do you ever try to do a bunch of tasks at once, thinking it's the best way to be super productive? Doing homework while listening to a podcast while checking Facebook means you're being productive, right? Think again.

You might call these collective activities "multitasking," but, realistically, it's more like trying to keep a dozen plates on sticks spinning at the same time without any of them falling and shattering. You're probably not doing your homework to the best of your ability if you're also doing several other things at the same time. Mindfulness is the rejection of the idea that you have to do it all and all at once. Remind yourself that you can actually get more done by focusing on one task at a time. Sure, it takes discipline, but your brain (and your report card) will thank you.

YOUR TURN

Multitasking is a hard habit to break, but it's not impossible! Fill out this information for a task you really need to get done, then silence your phone, stay off of YouTube, and do anything you need to in order to stay focused on this task for a certain period of time. After you've finished, reward yourself with something you held off on—checking your feeds, watching some videos, responding to texts, etc. Keep an eye on the clock and notice how long it takes you to progress through each project while "single tasking" instead of juggling everything at once. Did you save time? Was this hard to do? Keep practicing and it'll become second nature soon!

TASK THAT NEEDS TO GET DONE:

ESTIMATED TIME IT WILL TAKE:

HOW I'LL REWARD MYSELF WHEN I'M DONE:

ACTUAL AMOUNT OF TIME IT TOOK TO COMPLETE:

TASK THAT NEEDS TO GET DONE:

ESTIMATED TIME IT WILL TAKE:

HOW I'LL REWARD MYSELF WHEN I'M DONE:

ACTUAL AMOUNT OF TIME IT TOOK TO COMPLETE:

◆◆◆ AFFIRMATION ◆◆◆

*The task in front of me is my task at hand and
I will give it my undivided attention.*

Unplug and Relax on Vacation

Let's say you're lucky enough to be on spring break on a beach somewhere or up in the mountains, but instead of soaking up the sun or hitting the slopes, you're worried about finding the perfect Instagram shot or keeping up with the latest posts on TikTok. It's easy to think you have to capture and post key moments of your day, but that's just not true. Learning to detox from your phone, computer, or any other technology isn't just healthy; it's a necessity for your own mental well-being. Sure, it's fun to catch up with friends and share a choice picture or two from your vacation, but try thinking of how you're feeling during your vacation instead. Take in the sights and smells of the beach. Hear the seagulls crying, the waves crashing on the shore, and the vendors calling out. Being on social media takes you away from wherever you are, so try just being present. I promise, Snapchat will be there when you get back.

YOUR TURN

While it's incredibly tempting to post about your vacation on social media while you're experiencing it, one mindful baby step to separate yourself from social media during your vacation is to think about all the small details of what you're experiencing.

In the Instagram post outline, draw an image of your latest (or current) vacation and write a caption that embodies everything you heard, saw, smelled, tasted, and felt during this scene. The next time you go on vacation and have the urge to post about it on social media, create a post like this one that embodies a more mindful approach to the moment. Try your best to wait to post online until you get back home!

New Post

‹   Share

◆ ◆ ◆ **AFFIRMATION** ◆ ◆ ◆

I put down my phone and use my senses to experience what's around me.

Shut Off Your Phone

You probably don't remember a time when smartphones didn't exist, and you likely figured out all the ins and outs of the latest iPhone well before your parents did. You're probably a pro at finding the best Snapchat filter and swiping through TikTok in your downtime, but one thing you probably don't do is turn off your phone. Most people don't! It's your gathering space and social connector, and if you cut yourself off, what might you miss out on?!

Despite what you might feel, it's okay to be unavailable to your friends sometimes. With your parents' permission, take a walk and leave your phone behind or grab a burger with a friend and power down your phone. You—and your device—deserve a break.

YOUR TURN

When was the last time you spent time away from your phone, or even turned it off completely? Make a promise to yourself to spend at least thirty minutes each afternoon this week with your phone completely turned off. You'll be okay, I promise! Write down your feelings before and after you shut off your phone. At the end of the week, reflect on what you wrote. How did you feel? Did you notice any differences after creating that space and separation from your phone?

MISSION: SHUTTING OFF MY PHONE

DAY	SHUTTING MY PHONE OFF		TURNING MY PHONE BACK ON	
	TIME	HOW I FELT	TIME	HOW I FELT

Avoid the Comparison Trap and Know That You Are Enough

When you scroll through social media, it's easy to think that everyone else has a much better life than you. Aiden just had one of his videos go viral on TikTok, Mark scored tickets to the Super Bowl, and Ellie's parents are taking her to Europe next month to visit relatives. Meanwhile, you're stuck at home with nothing new or exciting happening. It's so easy to tie your self-worth into what you see on your screen, but what you see is far from the truth. While it may seem like Aiden, Mark, and Ellie have it made, what they're not posting is probably more telling. They almost certainly have many of the same fights with their parents, worries about school, and fears about the future that you have. Your self-worth is NOT tied to your social media feed or how people around you are living their lives. You are enough.

YOUR TURN

What exactly makes you think you're not good enough? This feeling often originates from outside influences, and identifying those influences will help you become aware of your negative thoughts and refute them. For example, you might be reading news stories that put down your generation, comparing your Instagram feed to someone else's, or feeling judged by family members, neighbors, or acquaintances. Be honest with yourself and write down some of these thoughts. Look at what you wrote and, one by one, cross them out. Under these crossed-out thoughts, write: I AM ENOUGH. Write this phrase over and over until you start to feel it in your heart. You're a wonderful person, and you truly are more than enough.

~~My sneakers are a generic brand.~~

I AM ENOUGH.

◆◆ **AFFIRMATION** ◆◆

I will not let comparison traps on social media make me feel less than what I am. I am enough.

Overcome FOMO

FOMO (fear of missing out) isn't unique to modern times, but apps like Instagram and Snapchat do make it more immediate and pervasive. Everyone posts about their adventures online, so now there's solid proof of who's there and who's not. At its root, the fear of missing out stems from the idea that this party/concert/show/event will be the best thing ever, and if you aren't there, your social life will be over.

Spoiler alert: That's not the case! Sure, there are some things you shouldn't miss (like your cousin's wedding or your best friend's birthday party, for instance), but, in general, no one event is that big a deal. Use mindfulness to assess how you're feeling in the present moment. If you'd prefer to spend your Friday night reading a book rather than going to a party, do it. Don't think about what you might miss by not going but rather about what you'll gain by staying. Use FOMO to your advantage by thinking of why exactly you're afraid to miss out on something and using it as an opportunity to grow.

YOUR TURN

Have you ever experienced FOMO? Jot down some thoughts about three events you didn't go to or weren't invited to in the left-hand circles. How did you react to discovering you weren't included in an event, or how did you feel about one you skipped? Think back to those nights—do you remember what you did instead? Did you enjoy yourself? Draw symbols of what you did instead in the right-hand circles. Do these symbols represent something important to you—your values or ways you enjoy spending your time? Celebrate these interests instead of focusing on the events you didn't go to. The next time you feel like you're missing out on something you see online or hear about later, think about the symbols you drew and remind yourself that, as long as you're following your values and what's fun to you, you're not truly missing out on life.

EVENT I DIDN'T ATTEND

WHAT I DID INSTEAD

◆ ◆ · AFFIRMATION · ◆ ◆

When I focus on what I'm missing, I fail to focus on what I have.

Live Without Regrets

Have you ever heard the phrase *carpe diem*? It's Latin for "seize the day," which is sometimes interpreted as "living life with zero regrets" or "risking it all for doing something fun and crazy." At its core, carpe diem is about making the most of an opportunity or doing something you otherwise wouldn't thanks to taking fear out of the equation.

It's powerful to imagine what you would do if you lived your life without regrets. Maybe you'd try to repair a friendship that's fallen to the wayside or reach out to someone in a different social circle without fear of rejection or mockery. When you calmly think about life's potential, it's easy to put fear and regret on the backburner.

YOUR TURN

On a scale of one to ten, how often do you think you seize the day and live your life without regrets? Circle your answer.

1 2 3 4 5 6 7 8 9 10
HARDLY AT ALL   *(Circle your answer)*   ALL THE TIME

Now think about where you put yourself on the scale—are you happy with this number? Do you wish you were a bit more adventurous and daring, or a little less? Why do you think this is? If you feel like you need to change because of society's opinions of what you *should* do, be mindful of that "should" and gracefully let it slip away.

If you'd like to move higher on the carpe diem scale because you truly believe you need to face your fears more often, write down three things you've always been scared to do. Are you afraid of snakes? Raising your hand in class? Once you've identified three, choose one to focus on and brainstorm ways you'll face this fear this week.

THREE THINGS I'M AFRAID TO TRY

1 _____

2 _____

3 _____

WAYS I COULD FACE MY FEARS

1 _____

2 _____

3 _____

✦ ✦ ✦ AFFIRMATION ✦ ✦ ✦

Focusing on the here and now, I leave regrets behind and embrace the richness life has to offer.

Be Safe and Smart Online

So much of our life takes place online these days. You can order groceries, hang out with friends, and you're probably expected to do a lot of your homework online too. But although all of this is second nature to us, there are still dangers to it. Much like you wouldn't try driving for the first time on a twelve-lane expressway, you shouldn't delve into the fast lane of the Internet without knowing what you're doing. Information is so easy to transmit these days, and you don't want to post compromising information—like a picture of your house with the address clearly visible or a part of your body that's private—online for the world to see.

YOUR TURN

The next time you're about to post something, take a minute to go through the following checklist beforehand. And don't be afraid to push yourself beyond this list and really think about if what you're posting should be online or not. If you answer "yes" to any of these questions then check the box next to it, and if you even debate a "yes" before switching to "no," it might be best to skip the post.

SAFE-TO-POST
CHECKLIST

- Is your personal information or safety at all exposed in this post?

- Will anyone (including you) get hurt by it?

- Is this image embarrassing for anyone pictured?

- Does this show any illegal activities (which shouldn't be happening anyway!)?

- Could this post affect your ability to get a job someday?

- If one of your friends or someone you knew wanted to post this, would you tell them not to?

Any boxes checked?

SKIP IT!

No boxes checked?

POST IT.

✦✦ **AFFIRMATION** ✦✦

Thinking before acting is the best way to keep myself and those around me safe online.

Consider Who You Are Online

Social media is a big part of life nowadays. Companies hire bloggers and influencers to promote jeans, makeup, and sports drinks on their social media channels. Friends' faces, meanwhile, are filtered and edited to extremes so as not to show a single pore or blemish, and makeup companies have started marketing "filter" makeup for the same reason. The larger message? That your online persona should be flawless and your life curated and perfect.

But that's far from reality. Life is messy and often difficult, but we don't typically see this reflected in social media. The real you is beautiful, and sometimes sharing the realness of you and your everyday life can help others feel more at ease and comfortable with who they are as well. The next time you post online, try to think about whether or not it reflects your most honest, genuine self. You don't need a drastic filter or to manipulate your body to be beautiful!

YOUR TURN

How much do you tweak your photos before posting them online? Do you use filters or apps like Facetune to change the way you look, or something else? If you frequently alter your photos before you post online (most people do, don't worry!), take a moment to really think about why you edit your photos so much. Are you unhappy with the way you look? Are you trying to prove something to or impress other people? Be honest with yourself; it's okay.

To start posting online without filters and editing, try the following baby steps, and remind yourself that everything about you makes you wonderful, beautiful, and uniquely YOU.

FOUR STEPS *to*
Posting <u>Without</u> Filters

1
If you usually use apps to alter your face or body, try to use one less tool on your next photo. For example, if you normally whiten your teeth and smooth out your skin, try to only use one of those editing features on your next picture.

2
Continue to use fewer editing features until you're no longer manipulating yourself to look different.

3
Try some simple edits next time, such as brightness or contrast to simply adjust lighting, rather than a huge overhaul to make your images look completely different.

4
Continue to shrink your use of filters and adjustments one by one, until you're posting a raw and authentic photo of the beautiful person you are right now.

Every time you post, remind yourself that you're amazing just the way you are!

◆ ◆ AFFIRMATION ◆ ◆
Instead of making it appear like my life is something it's not, I'll be genuine and courageous.

Look Beyond the Numbers

It's easy to get tied up in numbers—how many people you follow, how many follow you, how many likes or comments you get—but think about how many of those people you actually interact with in a real way. Is it a small number? If you think of how many you interact with on a daily basis, the number is probably smaller still.

So why does it really matter that you have a thousand followers on Instagram? How many of those people would you confide in if you were having a crisis? Instead, take stock of the richness of your friendships—the people who are there for you through thick and thin. True, this number might not be all that impressive to the casual observer, but wouldn't you rather have a handful of great friends than an army of people who only "like" you?

YOUR TURN

List the three most important people in your life and draw little images of them or the values they represent to you. Whether friends or family, they should be people who are there for you when times get tough or who you know you can turn to when you need a smile.

Focus on the people you just drew while breathing deeply. Feel their love and support and experience deep gratitude that they hold such a special place in your heart. The next time you find yourself caught up in caring about how many people liked your video or follow your account, remember these faces and feel that deep gratitude and love to conquer any insecurities that arise from worrying about numbers!

(Write name here)

(Write name here)

(Write name here)

◆ ◆ ◆ **AFFIRMATION** ◆ ◆ ◆

_The quality of my friendships—not their quantity—
helps shape my self-worth._

Use Your Vacation Wisely

After months of anguished waiting and counting down the days, it's finally here: summer vacation! Papers, tests, and heavy backpacks are swapped for flip-flops and beach towels. But hang on a second. Even if you have the luxury of a summer free of obligations like work or summer school, you shouldn't just fritter away your days. That can lead to—you guessed it—regret once the school year starts again.

Plant some seeds for your future by thinking of ways to give back to and/or enrich yourself. Maybe it's volunteering a day or two a week at an animal shelter, helping out with your library's summer reading program, or picking up a few odd jobs around the neighborhood to earn a little extra spending money. An active mind is a healthy one, and though it may seem like unnecessary work, it will benefit you in the long run.

YOUR TURN

Think about your goals for the future. Is there anything you're working toward that would benefit from dedicating some time to it this summer to help get you closer to your goal? Maybe you're eyeing a prestigious college that admires volunteer work, or you're saving up for your first big purchase. What's one thing you can do this summer to help you move closer to these dreams? Try your best to be mindful of your time during your next vacation and include some activities that help you work toward the bigger picture.

DREAM #1

DREAM #2

DREAM #3

Imagine Your Next Ten Years

Want to blow your mind? Think of where you'll be in ten years. You could be graduating college and thinking about your next steps. Maybe you'll be considering an advanced degree, getting your first internship, landing a job, or even moving to a new city.

Sure, it can be scary to think about, but it's also pretty exciting! You've probably thought a little (or maybe even a lot) about what you want to do after high school, but now's a good time to think more about yourself and your interests so you approach your future mindfully instead of just falling into whatever the people around you are doing. Yes, it's a little paradoxical to be talking about using mindfulness—which is rooted in the here and now—to chart your future ambitions, but look at it as more of an inner exploration. Asking yourself "Who am I?" and "What do I want to do with my future?" can help you develop a better picture of where you'll be in a decade.

YOUR TURN

In this picture, write down everything that comes to mind when you ask yourself "Who am I?" Answers can be simple, like "I'm a girl who loves to read," or something deeper, like "I value family and relationships above all else." There are no wrong answers!

Now, in the thought bubble near your head, fill in all your answers to the question "What do I want to do with my future?" Don't put too much pressure on yourself for this one. It's okay if you don't have it all figured out right now. Goals both big and small are allowed. Having some ideas and big dreams is a great place to start when it comes to shifting gears for the next phase of your life.

WHAT DO I WANT TO DO WITH MY FUTURE?

WHO AM I?

· ◆ · **AFFIRMATION** · ◆ ·

Looking inward, I can see my greatness. Looking outward, I plan my steps.

215

Prepare for College

It may seem light-years away, but the truth is, if you haven't already, you'll soon be getting information pamphlets in your mailbox and making visits to the lecture halls and tree-lined streets of college campuses. Thinking about getting into college can be really stressful. Maybe your parents are pushing hard for you to get good grades or to participate in a bunch of extracurricular activities to impress the admissions boards. It's true that applying to colleges can be stressful, but what matters most is finding your own path.

Try approaching each moment as it comes. It's all about knowing what you want out of your college experience. Maybe it's a big state school with 30,000 classmates or a tiny liberal arts college where you can pursue pottery making. Whatever the case, use mindfulness as your secret weapon to take things one step at a time.

YOUR TURN

Are you feeling overwhelmed by the pressure to do everything perfectly in order to get into the school of your choice? Use the space here to vent. Brain dump literally everything going on in your head. Now that you've poured out your swirling thoughts, it's time to clear your head a bit more. Close your eyes and take five deep breaths in, and out. Focus only on your breathing as much as possible, but if your mind wanders, that's okay! Gently bring it back to your breath. Feeling better?

The next time you feel like the stress is starting to become too much, try these two steps again to help clear your head. Focus only on what you can handle right now in this moment.

COLLEGE BRAIN DUMP

✦ ✦ ✦ AFFIRMATION ✦ ✦ ✦

With all the outside opinions and pressures in the world, I remember to stay true to myself and follow the path that feels right for me.

217

Discover Your Passion

Your middle school and high school years are some of the most difficult, hilarious, crazy, terrible, and amazing years of your life. On top of these experiences, you're also dealing with the fact that you have tons of big decisions to make. It can be overwhelming, like trying to climb a Mount Everest made of quicksand. But, by living your life in the moment, you can climb the mountain, step by step.

Discovering your passions can seem overwhelming too, but this just means identifying what you truly love to do. However, don't expect to wake up one day and know exactly who you are and what you want to do. It's a gradual process that takes time and thoughtfulness. By giving yourself time to think and assess daily, you'll find a richer, deeper passion than you would by simply stumbling along.

YOUR TURN

You may have a passion you're already enjoying but don't yet realize its potential, or there's one just waiting for you to discover it. Try this exercise:

In the hearts on the next page, write down everything you love or enjoy doing. This can be a hobby, favorite movie, absolutely anything! For each heart, write on the lines how that activity makes you feel. For example, if you love to draw, how do you feel when you're sketching?

When you're finished, take a look at your brainstorm. Which activity has the strongest emotions? That one has a high chance of being your passion! If there's more than one with similar feelings, that just means you might have more than one passion!

THINGS I LOVE

◆ ◆ ◆ AFFIRMATION ◆ ◆ ◆

*I listen to my heart and am open to discovering
all the things I'm passionate about in life.*

Pursue Your Purpose

Figuring out what you want to do with your life is kind of like the difference between being lost in the woods at night while barefoot and having a GPS to find your way out while wearing the best hiking boots and using a powerful flashlight. With the right tools and preparation, you move confidently, swiftly, and with a newfound sense of meaning and power. Finding your purpose is similar, but it's not something you can rush.

Whether your passion is studying the ocean floor or finding a cure for cancer, it often requires long hours, tough choices, and a lot of grit, but it's always worth it if it's what you really want to do. If you picture your life and can't imagine it without that aspect in it, you've got a purpose! Confidently pursue your goal, realizing that, with each step, you'll be in a better place than you were just a single step before.

YOUR TURN

If you're not sure what your purpose is, take a look at the passions you discovered in the previous entry. Write them down in the column on the left. For the right column, think of some ways you can turn that passion into a bigger purpose to impact the world around you. For example, if you're passionate about animals, maybe your purpose is to volunteer at a local animal shelter or to become a veterinarian!

Once you discover a purpose, think about the steps you can take to pursue it. You don't have to make huge strides right now. Small steps over time can have a huge impact on helping you achieve your biggest dreams. Each week, write down one thing you can focus on to help you pursue your purpose. Feeling stuck or unmotivated? Close your eyes and visualize yourself living your purpose and how it would feel to be in that moment. Bring that feeling and drive to the present and take the steps necessary to get closer to fulfilling your wildest dreams!

MY PASSIONS	IDEAS FOR A PURPOSE

ABOUT THE AUTHOR

SARA KATHERINE is a self-discovery coach and marketing manager who strives to help those who are overwhelmed find clarity and confidence, and integrate self-care into their daily lives. She has written three books, including *I'm Awesome. Here's Why…*; *Sara Earns Her Ears*; and *Be Happy. Be Calm. Be YOU*. Born and raised in California, Sara also loves creative writing, binge-worthy shows on Netflix, practicing yoga, and snuggling with her cat, Mochi. You can find Sara at Sara-Katherine.com and on Instagram at @sarakatherineblog.